"'Story' as a market[ing tool] has been explored to death, but [in a landscape where] influencers, and organizations feel the pressure to constantly create content, storytelling is a skill we need more than ever (and yet so many companies are still doing it poorly!). Thankfully, Carnes brings something refreshing and new to the conversation with clear and concise language (and great stories!) to help you not only effectively market your organization using the story cycle but to truly change the lives of your customers along the way."

—Hudson Phillips,
Screenwriter & founder of ScriptBlast

"In *The Story Cycle*, Robert Carnes reminds us of a timeless truth that we often forget: stories are not only core to the human experience, but also the lifeblood of any organization doing work that matters. Using one story after another, the reader is left not only inspired, but equipped to journey deeper into intentional storytelling themselves. I'm eager to employ the lessons learned to capture the attention of our customers and the hearts of our employees."

—Jamie Howard,
Slingshot Swag and co-author of
The Polaris-Away

"With varying results, organizations are increasingly leveraging stories to get our buy-in. But why are some stories more effective than others? Most of us aren't sure why, we just know they are. Robert Carnes in *The Story of Cycle*, makes it crystal clear why some stories positively impact us while others don't. But he does something deeper, something better. He isn't simply helping our organizations tell better stories, he helps us do it for a better reason, helping others. While the shift is subtle, it's powerful and ultimately is better for all of us. Read this book, it will not only help your organization tell better stories, it will also help be a better organization."

—Ted Lowe,
Speaker, Author, and
Founder of MarriedPeople.org

"*The Story Cycle* is a great guide to storytelling filled with a fresh perspective and engaging writing. Carnes shares wonderful insight that all organizations can benefit from."

—Vanessa Chase Lockshin,
Author of *The Storytelling Nonprofit*

"The term 'story' is ubiquitous in our world. Whether you lead a business, nonprofit, or athletic organization, telling your story in a clear, concise, and compelling fashion is paramount to your success. But how do you do this? Robert answers that question and demystifies the story process. Better storytelling means more profit, more customers, and more influence. And who wouldn't want that?"

—Brian Dodd,
Leadership Blogger and Author of *Timeless* and
2021 The Year In Leadership

"At Make-A-Wish, storytelling is the most powerful tool we have for engaging our supporters by creating an emotional journey that demonstrates the impact a wish creates for children with critical illness. *The Story Cycle* will teach you a framework for doing just that—and create a consistent process for developing story ideas for your organization's different audiences. The strategies in this book can help you connect to each of your audiences at different phases of their relationship with your organization."

—Jono Smith,
Head of Brand Communications &
Digital at Make-A-Wish America

"Robert has a unique viewpoint of the world, which he translates into straightforward writing to convey ideas and stories. That gift is helpful when explaining complex topics to an audience. I've worked directly with Robert and have seen the business impact of his storytelling."

—Grant Glas,
Founder & CEO of Playlister and
App Press

"How do you stand out in a noisy world and get someone's attention? In this book, you'll learn how to differentiate your organization through storytelling, share this message with your ideal customers, and better position yourself in the marketplace."

—Jesse Wisnewski,
Director of Marketing at PhoneBurner and
the co-author of *Read to Lead*

()

THE
STORY
CYCLE

YOUR BUSINESS GUIDE
TO BETTER MARKETING

ROBERT CARNES

LUCIDBOOKS

To Elise
I'm thankful to be able to watch your story
from the beginning.

TABLE OF CONTENTS

"Marketing is no longer about the stuff you make
but the stories you tell."

—Seth Godin

"A whole new cycle of stories waiting to be made."

—Robert Jordan,
The Eye of the World

FOREWORD

H ave you faked a leg injury for a marketing campaign? Hulk Hogan has.

It's 1990. Thanks to the expansion of pro wrestling and the film Rocky III, Hogan is a megastar worldwide. He encourages the millions of Hulkamaniacs to train, say prayers, and take vitamins.

He winds up in a feud with another wrestler named Earthquake. It's the typical formula: good guy (Hogan) versus bad guy (Earthquake). People love the good guy. They despise the bad guy. A good guy does good guy things. The bad guy does bad guy things.

It's a familiar refrain.

In the middle of the feud, Earthquake supposedly breaks Hogan's leg. Millions of distraught fans do what they're told to do next: write letters to their beloved Hulk Hogan as he "recovers."

This begs a question: why did the World Wrestling Federation fake a broken leg for their top star? Because it galvanized fans and made them take action.

And in 1990, a letter-writing campaign built your mailing list. Build your mailing list and you have a bigger audience to sell merchandise, videos, and so much more.

Remember: wrestling is scripted. Matches are predetermined. Wrestlers get people to believe they're the good guy or the bad guy. Tickets sell. Ratings soar. Money flows. All because of one thing: story.

Humans are wired for stories. It's why we binge-watch shows or see movies. Sure, we probably know how things end. Yet we watch because we love the way the story unfolds.

Here's a secret: your favorite movie or TV show follows a formula. It's not accidental. Each one follows old principles to get you to watch. And watch. And watch.

What does this mean for you? If you want to better engage an audience or build your brand, then study story. Learn how to use it well and unlock a powerful tool for growth.

Notice I didn't say tell stories. Instead, discover how story works. Learn the principles that make some stories great and others forgettable. If you want your brand to stand out and thrive, then pursue the art and science of story.

This book is a guide for understanding and using story. My friend Robert is both a student and a practitioner. Yes, he studies the concept of story and all its intricacies. But he also brings real-world experience using these concepts for brands and non-profits.

Use this book as a field guide to greater success. Follow the path Robert lays out and unlock a transformation in your business.

—Wes Gay
CEO of Wayfinder, a StoryBrand Certified Agency

INTRODUCTION

WHOSE STORY IS IT ANYWAY?

The Little Things

Once upon a time, it was all about the cows.

Those cows dominated Chick-fil-A's billboards, print ads, TV spots, and promotional items for several decades. Their adorably misspelled message to EAT MOR CHIKN worked. The Atlanta-based restaurant chain had grown into a highly-respected, multi-billion-dollar company.

Despite that success, the people who invented the chicken sandwich decided to make a change.

The cows are still around, but there are some non-bovine stars of Chick-fil-A's more recent TV commercials— people. Specifically, the customers and team members of the restaurants.

Chick-fil-A wanted to share the stories of the little ways their famous customer service has made a difference in their customers' lives. Stories like . . .

- A staff member in Topeka, Kansas saw a customer who was deaf and began signing with him, and became life-long friends.

- Or another worker in Columbia, South Carolina who showed a young man how to tie a necktie while his father was deployed overseas.

- Or the manager who extended the weekly family night by an extra hour to help a single mom give her kids a fun meal in Dumfries, Virginia.

- Or a franchise owner from Littleton, Colorado who protected customers under attack from a bird nesting in the restaurant parking lot using a big red umbrella.

More than two dozen of these 30-second stories have been aired. Each commercial features a few regular people having casual conversations while sitting on a red couch. Some of the stories are funny, some are emotional. Rarely do they mention a menu item, and the food itself isn't shown. Instead, the focus is on people and how they're impacted by simple, daily interactions.

Chick-fil-A's website shares its reasons behind these ads: *"To us, these are the people and the moments that make living and working in your communities so special. We hope you enjoy these stories as much as we have."*[1]

If Chick-fil-A's creative cows helped to build their brand, these 'Little Things' stories are the resulting impact of the brand they've built. Your brand isn't what your company says it is—your brand is what your audience says it is. That's a subtle but important shift for any business to make.

---

1   The big stories behind the 'little things', (Mar 19) [https://thechickenwire.chick-fil-a.com/inside-chick-fil-a/the-big-stories-behind-the-little-things]

2

And it's a shift that the chicken sandwich maker understands.

Former Chick-fil-A marketing chief Steve Robinson discusses marketing and storytelling in his 2019 book *Covert Cows and Chick-fil-A: How Faith, Cows, and Chicken Built an Iconic Brand*. From reading the book, it's clear that telling the story of great customer service has been baked into their brand from the very beginning.

A brand telling its own story is less powerful than when the customers or members of the media family tell those stories . . . I believed we would never be able to tell stories that genuinely captured the heart and the values of Chick-fil-A through advertising and have them be credible.[2]

Chick-fil-A didn't build its business off of TV advertising; they built it off of outstanding customer service. That's what their brand is known for. It's what people think of when you mention Chick-fil-A. Then they created TV ads that allowed their customers to talk about it on national television. Robinson didn't think they could find the same credibility through ads, but they managed it because they elevated the voices and stories of their community.

These simple 30-second commercials exemplify an elusive skill that some companies get right, but far more fail to understand—**the stories we tell aren't about us, they're about the people we serve**. When we serve them well, they reward us by trusting us with even more stories to share.

Luckily for us, stories don't close on Sundays.

---

2   *Covert Cows and Chick-fil-A: How Faith, Cows, and Chicken Built an Iconic Brand*, Steve Robinson, page 81 (2019)

Meet The Story Cycle

To discover this new way of looking at business storytelling, we'll examine a concept that I've compiled from my research and experiences. You can call it a framework, a theory, or a joke. But I tend to call it The Story Cycle.

In the first three chapters of this book, we'll examine what we mean when we talk about stories.

- That starts by recognizing, despite what we may think, that not everything is a story.

- This leads us to question what characteristics make a true story.

- Then we'll consider an unusual (maybe crazy) idea—that stories are living things, with lifespans and deaths of their own.

- This gives us the power to better extend the lives and impact these stories have.

Then we'll examine the two players in the Story Cycle—our organization and our intended audience. It's not enough just to realize these two players exist, but to understand our different roles in the story process. **Storytelling requires both your business and an audience**, like a game of catch between a pitcher and catcher.

From there, we'll walk through the six steps of the Story Cycle itself—three steps each for both our organization and the audience. These steps follow a clear sequence that keeps the Story Cycle spinning.

- Your organization must first capture a story,

- then craft it by assembling the pieces and editing them together
- before finally sharing the story with your audience.
- Once the audience experiences the story,
- they should be called to a clear and compelling action,
- to experience the life change that your organization offers.

Each of these chapters is sprinkled with real (and some fictional) examples of stories that companies tell and lessons we can apply in our work. **The best way to learn storytelling techniques is by learning from the example of others.** Besides, it makes for a more entertaining read.

Each chapter unpacks barriers that break the Story Cycle. These are the weak links in the chain that connect you to your audience. They're the landmines to avoid. If you don't pay attention to these pitfalls, your story likely won't hit its mark or survive through the entire Story Cycle.

This book is packed with practical advice because storytelling is too often theoretical and hard to grasp. **Storytelling is not just a mindset, but an art that must be studied, practiced, and refined over time.** We'll explore a variety of real-life stories and learn specific lessons from each.

- Why Greco-Roman mythology demonstrates how stories are living things.
- How millions of conversations between strangers help us find the right stories to tell.

- How a team of editors saved a galaxy far, far away, and what they learned could save your stories, too.
- What the original anti-conference can teach us about sharing stories.
- How a pitch-black traveling exhibit instills empathy and creates an unforgettable experience.
- What following a frog demonstrates about calling your audience to action.
- How a false newspaper headline inspired the most well-known prize and changed the world.

The ultimate goal is to outline a better storytelling process within your own business. Not just so you can grow your business, but so that you can use it to impact people for good. Because those are the kinds of businesses that have stories worth telling.

THE **STORY CYCLE**

Audience
(Hero)

Organization
(Guide)

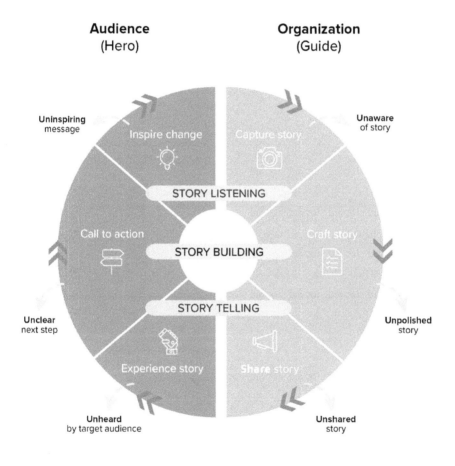

Uninspiring
message

Inspire change

Capture story

Unaware
of story

STORY LISTENING

Call to action

Craft story

STORY BUILDING

STORY TELLING

Unclear
next step

Unpolished
story

Experience story

Share story

Unheard
by target audience

Unshared
story

PART 1

3 UNREALIZED STORY TRUTHS

"The stories we tell literally make the world.
If you want to change the world, you need
to change your story. This truth applies both to
individuals and institutions."
—Michael Margolis,
CEO Storied, Educator, Anthropologist

CHAPTER 1

NOT EVERYTHING IS A STORY

Big Idea: Every true story has specific ingredients.

Not a Storytelling Machine

"Down every road is a story," begins the narrator. It opens with the image of a parachuting astronaut, followed by a man in a suit carrying a birdcage.

"The further you go, the more wild and unexpected they get."

Cut to a disco ball in the forest. And for some reason, a pinball machine in an otherwise empty alleyway. Then, finally, a car drives majestically along open, dirt roads.

"That's why, when we built the new Sorento, we didn't just build an SUV," concludes the unknown narrator's voice. "We built the world's first storytelling machine."

And fade to black.

That's the entirety of a new car commercial from Kia. That's right, it's official. The South Korean car-maker no longer makes cars—they build storytelling machines. Oh boy.

I understand what Kia is trying to do here. Car commercials have long drawn on the "find new adventures in your cool new car" motif. And it generally works fine. People can genuinely go on story-worthy journeys in a car. A decent all-terrain vehicle can help us achieve adventure or "find new roads," just like Chevy's commercials encourage us to do. But Kia's latest attempt at this trick is lazy. There's no central narrative to their ad. The random images don't make any sense. There's no opportunity for us to picture ourselves driving the vehicle. The audience isn't invited into the narrative.

Not to mention, what makes the Kia Sorento equipped to be "the world's-first storytelling machine"? There are at least a dozen other machines that can lay claim to that title: The television. The radio. The typewriter. There are now artificial intelligence programs that can be programmed to create their own stories.

A storytelling machine sounds like a cool name for a car. But you're required to tell the stories to back up that bold claim. **You've got to prove to your audience that you understand their story**. You must weave a narrative that drivers can see themselves inside. Unfortunately, Kia's new ad campaign does none of that.

Kia is desperately trying to convince their audience (and themselves) that by directly mentioning storytelling, they're telling a story. Their idea is valid, but it skidded off of the road due to poor maneuvering. And Kia's not alone. Plenty of business executives and advertising agencies have fallen into this same trap.

Mentioning storytelling does not automatically make it storytelling. **Storytelling is about more than just using the right buzzwords.** And not everything we tell is a story.

To prove my point, it's time for a pop quiz. Which businesses go with the following taglines:

- Telling the world's stories
- Opening hearts and minds, one story at a time
- We help you tell your story

None of these are bad taglines. They each go with good businesses, but they're each worryingly generic. Any one of these taglines could be attached to one of a hundred different companies. They're not unique to any of these distinct businesses. Granted, a little context might help.

Are you still wondering who these taglines match with and wish I would stop beating around the bush? "Telling the world's stories" is an advertising tagline of the streaming giant Netflix. "Opening hearts and minds, one story at a time" belongs to the movie theater chain Studio Movie Grill. And "We help you tell your story" matches up with the fundraising platform, Kickstarter.

Each of these businesses has storytelling woven into its DNA. Each tells stories in their own way—whether through streaming shows, projecting them on the big screen, or helping raise money for that bright new idea. However, each of these companies also understands that true storytelling requires more than just their tagline. It has to be an integral part of their brand.

The 4 Cs of Storytelling

Stories are universal. They're timeless. They're everywhere within our society, like Starbucks locations or true crime podcasts. **The frequency and excitement with which we talk about storytelling make it easy to believe that nearly everything you share is a story.** Some *would* argue that anything and everything is a story. Every time a business executive makes a speech during a board meeting, that's a story. Each time your company posts a meme on social media, it's a story. Every sales call you make to a potential customer, that's a story.

But that's not the case.

None of those things are automatically stories. They have the potential to be, but there are four common elements every true story contains. These characteristics set stories apart from boring anecdotes or never-ending yarns. They are the requirements for being considered a story.

1. Context

"You can still dunk in the dark."

Super Bowl XLVII was played on February 3, 2013, in New Orleans, LA., between the San Francisco 49ers and the Baltimore Ravens. It was the first Super Bowl in the Big Easy since Hurricane Katrina struck the city nearly eight years earlier. The game was a matchup between coaching brothers John and Jim Harbaugh. It was a competitive game, won by the Ravens by only three points, with a final score of 34-31.

That's the context for our story.

All of that was almost literally overshadowed by a technical malfunction at the Superdome. What most people will remember about that game was what happened with the lights. Right after the start of the third quarter, the power went out in the stadium.

Not Everything is a Story

For 34 awkward minutes, with the entire nation watching, the biggest football game of the year was paused. Players paced the field anxiously. Fans in the stands wondered why they'd spent so much money on tickets. Millions of viewers at home pulled out their cellphones (if they weren't out already) to check everyone else's reactions on social media.

Scrolling through Twitter during that half-hour, thousands of people saw a viral post from an unlikely source—Oreo. The tweet simply read: "Power out? No problem." Below that was a graphic with an Oreo cookie, a dark gradient, and the slogan: "You can still dunk in the dark."

Oreo captured more buzz and attention than all of the commercials during the Super Bowl because they reacted quickly and shared something contextually relevant.

In the tweet, there is no mention of the Super Bowl, football, or even specifically the blackout itself. But everyone who read it at the moment understood the context. It was like an inside joke that practically everyone was in on.

Oreo's Blackout Bowl tweet might not be an entire story,[3] but it shows the power of context within organizational storytelling. There's a fascinating story behind the story, too. Oreo partnered with marketing agencies 360i and MediaVest to make it happen. Together, they invested time into understanding their online audience so that the cookie company would be ready when the right storytelling opportunity opened up.

So when the lights went out during the Super Bowl, they

---

3   I'd argue that this example isn't a story because it doesn't meet my own rules for a story. But it's a really good example of organizational context— so it at least fits one criterion.

were ready to strike with a funny and contextually appropriate message.

Sometimes leveraging context means coming up with the right idea at the right time. Other times, that means providing context clues so people will understand what details are relevant. This requires knowing your audience and the medium you're using to share your story. But we'll unpack how to do that later in this book.

Every story has context because every story happens somewhere and some-when. Providing details about the time and place gives your audience a frame of reference. It's certainly possible to overshare contextual details, so consider what's relevant information for your audience to have. Perhaps you didn't need to know about the fun fact about John and Jim Harbaugh coaching against one another to get the message of this story—so I probably could have edited that out.

Like the Story Cycle itself, **a story's context is broken into two halves**: the internal and external context. The internal context is more recognizably referred to as the setting—the time, place, and circumstances that surround the narrative.

For external context, we're focused on two things: the platform used to share the story and the timing of when it's shared. We'll delve into the more practical aspects of how this comes into play later. For now, the important thing is to recognize the context of the stories you hear and tell.

Admittedly, understanding context is perhaps the easiest requirement for any story to meet. Even boring anecdotes happen somewhere. But it's crucial to know what details of context to include during the telling to make the story compelling to your intended audience.

2. Character

"Only you can prevent wildfires."

During World War II, most American firefighters were drafted into military service. Meanwhile, the Japanese navy launched a firebombing strategy aimed at the American west coast. Fearing an inability to combat dangerous wildfires, the U.S. Forest Service scrambled to form a new strategy for wildfire prevention.

Nine out of 10 wildfires are started by human causes,[4] so their goal was to educate individuals on their role in fire safety. The Forest Service knew they'd need a coordinated ad campaign to get out this message. And to make it stick with people, they'd need a face for the campaign.

For the first year of the campaign, Walt Disney loaned the government use of the animated characters from the newly-released film *Bambi*. The furry woodland creatures urged Americans to do their part. But the contract with Disney only lasted a year. The Forest Service was forced to develop a new character of its own.

To lead the charge against wildfires, they chose a fictional bear. An artist hired by the department sketched the grizzly wearing blue jeans and a park ranger hat. Thus, Smokey Bear was born.

The first Smokey Bear posters were introduced in August 1944. Three years later, they minted what would become Smokey's signature phrase: "Only YOU can prevent forest fires." Smokey began appearing in radio and television spots

---

4   Smokey Bear [https://www.stateforesters.org/smokey-bear/]

in the 1960s. Since then, the Smokey Bear campaign has gone on to become the longest-running PSA campaign in history.

More importantly, the Forest Service's campaign worked. There's no true way to measure the effectiveness of prevention. But brand awareness shows how pervasive Smokey has become in our culture. His look, his voice, and even his catchphrase has shifted over the years, but Smokey Bear is recognized by 95% of U.S. adults and 77% of children.[5]

Government ad campaigns aren't the only ones to use characters to embody their message. Mascots create a visual representation of a conceptual brand. The term "mascot" originates from the French word "mascotte," meaning a "lucky charm." Mascots represent everything from sports teams to companies. They're a way of personalizing a brand and creating a focal character for an organization's story. How a mascot looks, acts, and sounds like is meant to be a representation of what the company stands for.

That's why Chick-fil-A introduced some illiterate cows on their billboards and Dos Equis brought us "The Most Interesting Man in the World"—because they're someone we can focus on any time we think about chicken sandwiches or Mexican beer.

Every story needs a character. All stories happen to someone. In many cases, especially within the organizational setting, that someone turns out to be the person telling the story—but it doesn't have to. You can tell stories about someone else.

---

5   A History of the Most Iconic Brand Mascots Since 1877 [https://erinsweeneydesign.com/marketing/a-history-of-the-most-iconic-brand-mascots-since-1877/]

Tell the story of someone who the audience can resonate with. Find a character whose shoes the audience can see themselves in. That character is a stand-in for them, a perspective for them to see from. Focusing on a character gives the story a face that we can follow during the narrative.

3. Conflict

"The pizza was cardboard."

Domino's had a problem. Their pizza was widely panned (pun intended) for its inedible delivery pizza. The company was a household name, but its brand had become synonymous with bland food. Rather than sidestepping that criticism or sugarcoating it, Domino's owned the conflict.

They released a four-minute "documentary" called "The Pizza Turnaround" in December 2009. It began with clips highlighting the bad things people said about their food. Customers called it everything from inedible to cardboard. Basically, a food company's worst nightmare.

Domino's franchise owners and corporate employees couldn't argue with that customer consensus. Rather than fighting these comments or making excuses, they agreed with these negative criticisms. Domino's did something many businesses aren't secure enough to do—they publicly apologized, acknowledged their shortcomings, and vowed to fix the problem.

In the video, Domino's CEO J. Patrick Doyle said: "You can use negative comments to get you down or use it to excite and energize the process of making better pizzas. We chose the latter."

By not avoiding the truth, Domino's earned the trust to tell more of their story about how the pizza chain was founded on quality ingredients and tasty pies. But they also didn't shy away from admitting how they'd veered off of that path and were making changes to correct their course.

"The Pizza Turnaround" became the basis for a long-running ad campaign by Domino's to promote their newly-imagined food line that included more than just pizza. They attempted to take control of the narrative and start shifting how people thought about their brand.

A year after the pizza chain ran the ads, its stock price had increased by 130%. More importantly, the public sentiment toward their food balanced out the overwhelmingly negative feelings people held before. They saved themselves *from* themselves with honesty and ownership of their mistakes.

Conflict is inevitable in storytelling. Conflict is the fuel that makes stories go. Without tension, stories are just dead in the water. However, too many organizations neglect this fact—we shy away from conflict because we don't want to come across as negative.

Don't think of conflict in a story as a bad thing—remember that it's just the beginning of the narrative.

Just as stories can't exist without conflict, neither can your business. You're in the business of helping someone fix a problem. They pay you money because you can solve their challenge better than they could on their own—whether that's fixing a leaky toilet, filing their taxes, or making chew toys for their dog.

While not every corporate storytelling campaign needs to own direct conflict like Domino's did, we can still embrace the challenges that our audience faces. When we acknowledge the tension in their lives, we can potentially earn their trust in providing a solution.

4. Change

The Swiss-Army Knife of Companies

You might not immediately be familiar with Victorinox, but you've heard of their most famous product. The company was founded by Karl Elsener in 1892 out of his workshop in the small Swiss village of Ibach. A cutler by trade, Elsner made knives and sold them primarily to the Swiss military. That's what led Victorinox to promote their wares as the *Original Swiss Army Knife*. Over the years, they've adapted into their modern-day appearance: red, bearing the Swiss cross emblem and containing any number of handy devices like screwdrivers, nail files, and corkscrews.

By the turn of the twenty-first century, Victorinox was the largest seller of pocket knives in the world. Although there were a wide variety of Swiss Army knives, the product made up the vast majority of the company's sales. Then one day, everything changed. That day was September 11, 2001.

Overnight, potentially dangerous objects like pocket knives were prohibited on airplanes and some governmental buildings. Selling their wares in duty-free shops in airports, once a huge source of pocket knife sales, was now an impossibility. Airports returned thousands of knives. People stopped buying knives. The product that had carried them for over a century was no longer enough.

Victorinox's revenue dropped 40% instantly. The company that had built its business on the back of pocket-sized multi-tools was faced with a dilemma. But rather than buckle in the face of adversity, they pivoted. Just like their famous knives, they showed that they were multifaceted.

Just before 2001, Victorinox had experimented with a few other product lines—leisurewear, kitchen cutlery, luggage,

21

watches, and fragrances. Before being forced to change, this product diversification seemed like an unnecessary distraction from their core offerings. Now, those other products became a focus to stabilize the now floundering business. Victorinox had to fundamentally change the story they told the world about their offerings to survive. They had to show that they were more than just the people who made Swiss Army knives.

Four years later, Victorinox was surging back into success. They were in a good enough financial situation to acquire their largest rival, Wenger. Not only had they survived the curveball of 9/11, but they emerged even stronger than ever. A wider variety of products meant that they were able to grow and expand their brand beyond Swiss Army knives. If they hadn't been forced to change, who knows if that would have ever happened.

Victorinox is far from the only business to make a significant pivot in times of trouble. Marriott Hotels started as a root beer stand. The video game maker Sega began by producing slot machines in the 1940s until they were outlawed. 3M, the company that makes office supplies like Post-it notes, was originally founded as a mining company.

Effective stories feature change—whether that's a transformation in a character or a business. There should be some dynamic shift from the beginning of the narrative to the end. This change is usually a response to the story's conflict. A character has a desire, they're met with a conflict, and they're forced to change (internally, externally, or both) to overcome that challenge.

We're drawn to stories of dramatic change because they show us that we're capable of a similar transformation. These narratives resonate with us because we want to be inspired by their example.

Story Ingredients

These are the four Cs of any true story:

1. Context
2. Character
3. Conflict
4. Change

Every story will have different levels of each—some will focus more on conflict, and others will contain a heavier dose of character. But they should all be present to count. That's how you tell the difference between a story and just another anecdote.

Use these ingredients as your internal checklist before sharing any story. Checking for each of these pieces ensures that nothing is missing and strengthens the existing parts.

For example, it's easy to shy away from conflict in the stories we tell. Business leaders want the content we share to be positive, but conflict automatically feels negative. So, we often downplay any part that creates friction. Fight that urge. As we discussed in the Conflict section, this is the ingredient that provides a story's fuel. Conflict isn't always easy to spot either. But if you look for it in your organization, you'll also find opportunities for stories. Just don't forget to share the resolution to the conflict—for better or for worse.

What do you do if what you're about to share is missing ingredients? What if you just don't have any conflict, or there's no example of change? Perhaps that means you're not ready to share it yet. Look closely for where you might have missed those elements and see how highlighting them might strengthen your message.

Even if not everything is a story, it's OK to reconcile that **not everything *needs* to be a story**. You're allowed to give a speech or distribute marketing material that *doesn't* contain a story in it. Making everything at your company a story can dilute their power. Save those stories for the right audience at the right time. Only share stories that are worth telling.

Because, like it or not, the stories that are shared are the stories that continue to live on in our society. Meanwhile, the stories that aren't shared wither up and die. That's a fact of life—and the fact is **that stories have lives of their own.**

In Summary

- Stories are everywhere, but not everything is a story.

- True stories have specific characteristics that set them apart.

- Context provides a helpful framework for a narrative—because every story happens somewhere and some-when.

- Characters give a story a recognizable point of view for the audience to connect with—because every story happens to someone.

- Stories cannot exist without conflict—because that's the fuel that drives a narrative forward.

- Effective stories are examples of how a character change in the face of conflict—and the best stories are the ones that make us want to change, too.

CHAPTER 2

STORIES ARE LIVING THINGS

Big idea: Stories have a natural lifespan that depends on their impact.

It's All Greek Mythology to Me

The Roman Empire was really good at conquering places. They were like a violent amoeba—swallowing up entire civilizations and absorbing them into the Roman way of life.

As the Romans collected new territories, they took time to learn and assimilate parts of the native culture, this included new inventions, ideas, and even belief systems. As a pagan society, the Romans worshiped thousands of gods. They collected them like Pokémon cards. Many of these were adapted from other people groups across the known world.

The Romans were global story collectors. This both helped with managing the sprawl of their global empire, but it also fueled their march to gobble up even more cultural narratives.

By 146 BC, Rome controlled much of the Mediterranean region. They looked around and noticed they hadn't yet bothered to invade Greece. So, marching into the Grecian peninsula seemed like the next logical step. (Which the Greeks would know since they essentially invented logic.)

After conquering Greece, the Roman overlords allowed the deep-thinking Greeks to continue much of their way of life. Think of it as a hostile company acquisition, without forcing the Greeks to rebrand. But whether the Romans realized it or not, the Greek philosophy had more impact on the Roman Empire than either of them would realize.

In the end, it wouldn't be entirely clear who invaded who.

The Greek mythological canon is one of the most popular and influential collections of stories in the entire world, certainly in Western culture. Even thousands of years later, many modern people know the stories of Hercules, Achilles, Zeus, and all of the other Hellenic figures. Perhaps this is in part because of the longevity of the Greek way of thinking, but also the strength and dominance of the Roman Empire.

Famously, the Roman Empire took a particular liking to Greek mythology—to the point where many of the most well-known Roman gods and heroes were mild adaptations from similar Grecian stories. Hercules is the Roman name for the Greek hero Heracles. (The spelling is so similar, it's a rip-off; good thing the Greeks didn't invent copyright law.) Jupiter, Mercury, Pluto, and a few other planet eponyms were named after Zeus, Hermes, and Hades, respectively.

Even most of the stories involving these gods and heroes were closely based on Greek mythology. This makes sense because that's how myths and legends occur—organically shared from person to person, and generation to generation, slowly shaped and sculpted over the years. It only follows that these stories could just as easily be passed from one culture or country to the next.

Long after the Greeks fell subject to the Roman empire, long after the Greek philosophers died, and long after both Rome and Greece became religious centers of Christianity, the stories of the Greek myths endure. Today, we recognize these as fictional legends rather than spiritual truths. Not many people still worship Zeus or Apollo.[6] But the staying power and continued influence of these myths show that stories live on within people.

It wasn't just the Romans that the Greek myths infected with their influence—our modern society has been subject to that infestation as well. And it's not just the stories of Greek mythology that have pervaded American pop culture, too.

As far back as the 1940s, DC Comics have featured characters from Greek Mythology—Hades, Hermes, Zeus, and other ancient gods exist in the same superhero universe as Superman, Wonder Woman, and the Green Lantern. Their stories even made the jump to the big screen in 2017 when the Greek god of war Ares served as the villain in the DC film *Wonder Woman*.

Pop culture alone shows that our zeitgeist is inspired by stories first told thousands of years ago. Some stories have fleeting life spans that spark and flicker and fade. Other narratives catch fire and stay ablaze for longer than the civilizations that created them.

Stories Are Alive

Stories are living things. Not in the same way humans are, but they still have a life force.

---

6   Although there are still some. The religion they practice is usually referred to as Hellenism.

Beyond that, **stories have a symbiotic relationship with human beings**. In fact, they're borderline parasitic. They need people as a host to continue living. But they don't survive to our detriment. Quite the opposite—stories have always been beneficial for humans. They allow us to communicate, express, and understand complex ideas.

In sharing stories, we expand their life. **Every time a story is shared, it grows.** As long as a story is remembered, it lives on. As a story endures, it morphs and transforms. When you tell a friend a story, you infect their mind with a living story. The more influential the story or the more impassioned the telling, the deeper the story will take root in that person's mind and will likely be spread again.

Thankfully, this relationship is mutually beneficial. Stories help us make sense of the world. They entertain us, help us escape the stresses of life, and bring us inspiration. That's why we continue to share the best ones—**because stories enrich us as we enrich them**.

Stories have life stages and life cycles. Like all living things, some stories are short-lived. They barely reach infancy before being forgotten. On the other hand, a few stories reach immortal status and can exist indefinitely. That's one of the ways they're unique from actual living organisms. **As long as there are people to share them, there will be stories living within us**.

Viewing a story as a living thing helps us to more completely understand the role they play in our lives and cultures. It helps us see why some stories spread, while others die. This principle demonstrates why stories evolve and mean different things to different people. It also allows us to believe that great stories can inspire the birth of even more stories through the work of intentional practice.

That's the foundational belief behind the Story Cycle.

Monkeying Around with Stories

There's a scripted comedy series that imagines what it's like to create those cheesy stock photos everyone hates using. Then there's a mockumentary about trade shows and the ridiculous people who travel to them to hawk their even more ridiculous products. You can't forget the docu-series about remote workers in constant search for Wi-Fi. Or the short film about students learning the delicate art of noodle making.

These are actual descriptions of the more than 30 different original pieces of content created by Mailchimp Presents—the in-house content studio of Mailchimp, the marketing software company. This content includes a mix of limited-run shows, short films, podcasts, and documentaries—all aimed at telling the stories of small businesses and entrepreneurs. Each of the pieces of content is short because they know that their audience is busy.

"We're really trying to create stories that speak to the themes of what it feels like to be an entrepreneur and what that journey is really like," said Mark DiCristina, head of Mailchimp studios. "There's not really a lot of that kind of content in the world."[7]

Since originally launching the "business entertainment platform" back in 2019, Mailchimp Presents has slowly

---

7   Mailchimp Presents to feature original programming to inspire entrepreneurs, The Drum, by Kyle O'Brien (June 11, 2019) [https://www. thedrum.com/news/2019/06/11/mailchimp-presents-feature-original-programming-inspire-entrepreneurs]

added to its library of content, spending millions of dollars to intrigue, inform, and entertain potential new customers.

It's an interesting and risky investment because there's no guarantee that a funny internet show will convince you to use Mailchimp's product—especially since none of the content is about or even mentions the company that made it.

Mailchimp hasn't stopped their more traditional advertising—with magazine ads and billboards. But they rely heavily on this indirect form of story marketing to grow their brand interest.

Here's something else to consider. Not all of the businesses featured in their stories are real. Many are, but a handful of the content is completely fictional. The videos are professionally scripted and acted, similar to a Netflix show. It's pretty clear which content is fiction, so it's not an attempt to manipulate. **But can fictional stories work for a business?**

That depends. A growing tech company like Mailchimp with resources to burn has the capability of creating and distributing quality fictional content. Developing original content in-house isn't new for larger corporations, especially technology and entertainment-focused businesses.

However, smaller businesses don't have the same luxury. The rest of us have the privilege of telling true stories—narratives about our customers with our organization as a supporting character. It's tougher for the average company to justify commissioning fictional content. Not because fiction stories aren't important. But there's a longer path to a return on your investment.

After all, there's a fundamental difference between fictional stories and the real stories told by your organization.

The Power to Change the World

Ideas have power. They move people to action, and enough people sharing the same idea can create communities or destroy empires. These ideas can come from inspirational leaders or innovative businesses. Occasionally, these world-changing ideas come from fictional stories. But more often they come from the true stories we share.

As entertaining and inspiring as the *Harry Potter* books or the Marvel Cinematic Universe might be, they don't fundamentally alter our lives. They don't drastically change how we see the world. They don't necessarily help us to live a better life—other than maybe the momentary escape from it. Fictional stories are powerful, but that influence only extends so far.

True stories, on the other hand, have a greater power to change the world.

Your organization's stories won't be as groundbreaking as Plato's *Republic* or as controversial as *The Origin of the Species* or as influential as the Bible. Thankfully, they probably won't be as gruesome as true crime stories.

But they still have one thing in common—they're true. That truth carries an undeniable power. Your creative energies won't focus on creating a fictional world or character; instead, you have the opportunity to share the real story of actual people and events. You have the privilege of potentially shaping real people and events as a result.

What stories do organizations like yours have to tell? How can businesses harness this tremendous and tenuous power? In the next chapter, we'll examine how businesses can set their audience up as the hero of the story by establishing themselves as the guide.

In Summary

- Stories are living things that are born and have life spans. Unlike the people who create them, stories can endure forever by being shared.

- When most people hear storytelling, they think of fictional stories—novels, movies, and theater. However, nonfiction narratives can be equally as potent.

- Most businesses don't tell fiction stories. We must rely on telling the true stories of the people involved in our organization.

- Both real and invented stories have the power to change the world. But nonfiction stories provide businesses with more opportunities to do so.

CHAPTER 3

YOU'RE NOT THE
HERO OF THE STORY

Big idea: Your organization isn't the hero of the story—you get to be the guide for your audience.

Two Halves of the Story Cycle

There's a difference between fictional and non-fiction stories. In the same way, there is a difference between the stories we tell as individuals and those we collectively tell as organizations. Sure, companies can use made-up stories in advertising or marketing pieces. But these narratives must be grounded in reality and truth for them to resonate with the target audience.

Novelists have the freedom to create any story they can imagine. On the other hand, organizations have the responsibility of nurturing real stories. These true stories don't always fit neatly into a plot, but they can nevertheless inspire and entertain. But just like with fictional stories, that's not always easy and it comes with practice and patience.

One of the primary distinctions between fictional and organizational stories is the audience. For fiction writing, the audience is only the group that encounters and enjoys a story. For the stories told by a brand, however, the audience can be both the recipient and the subject of the story. **Businesses that tell compelling stories about their customers will likely attract more customers.** And therefore, they'll have more stories to tell. That's the core concept within the Story Cycle. Stories are the connective tissue between a company and its customers. It's the most ideal way for brands and their audience to communicate with one another.

For this reason, the Story Cycle is broken into two halves: the organization and the audience. Too often, storytellers focus on the organizational half. We think about what it takes to create and share an impactful story. Then we forget about it. But that is a mistake. That's why we struggle to find more ideas for our stories. Because we aren't looking at the best source—our audience.

Keeping the cycle flowing is what keeps good stories alive. Not only that, but it gives birth to other great stories. When you realize this core idea, organizational storytelling will become more natural and the foundation for your marketing and sales. That's because you'll learn that effective storytelling is a lucrative way to grow a business or share an idea.

Like Moths to Flame

George Green grew up on St. Simon's Island, a small barrier island in South Georgia, near the Florida border. He spent late evenings with a small group of friends drinking whiskey and swapping stories on a friend's front porch in the sticky summer heat.

One of the most vivid memories he had of these times was the moths drawn toward the evening porch lights. They found themselves similarly drawn to stories—the characters, the adventures, the tensions. So, the group called themselves The Moths.

Green suffers from a rare condition known as hypernychthemeral syndrome, meaning that his body operates on a 25-hour cycle unlike everyone else. People with the condition sleep for eight hours a day and then stay awake for the next 17 to 18 hours. This gradually puts them out of sync with the rest of society.

This made traditional education difficult for Green, so he dropped out of high school. But he was able to hold down jobs in security and construction while working on poetry and novels.

In 1997, Green was a budding novelist with two books already published—both of which would be adapted to the big screen. He moved to New York City to pursue a literary career but missed those summer nights sharing stories with The Moths. So, he set about recreating the same experience in the Big Apple.

He invited some new friends to his New York living room. There were only two rules about the stories: they had to be true and they had to be about you. Through word of mouth, the events grew. More people were invited to subsequent storytelling events to the point where they had to move to larger Manhattan venues. As they grew, organizers began selling tickets and put together a prepared program with invited storytellers on a formal stage.

"Everyone who goes up says it's probably the scariest and most profound experience of their lives," says Green. "Because they suddenly have this very simple connection with a group of people where they're just telling them who they are . . . but it's not just coming through their words, it's coming through every pore of their body."[8]

The Moth story slams have since spread to 29 cities around the world. Over 30,000 stories have been shared at more than 500 live shows each year. Each event features 10 speakers chosen at random telling five-minute stories to a packed crowd. These gatherings are based around an open-ended theme and are unscripted.

Not only that, but The Moth also runs storytelling workshops for students and adults through their community outreach programs. Beyond the live shows, The Moth produces a popular podcast and a weekly Moth Radio Hour broadcasted on more than 480 radio stations around the globe.

More than just storytellers, Green describes participants in The Moth shows as 'raconteurs.' A raconteur is someone skilled at sharing anecdotes. But the size and scope of The Moth show that there is power in these simple anecdotes.

"There aren't any more fun nights to be had," Green said, "than gathering with your friends, drinking and listening to stories."

Your Audience as The Hero

The Moth provides a powerful example of the audience as a player in the Story Cycle. Organizational stories do not exist without an audience. Not only are they the people who hear

---

8   The Times, August 8, 2009 [http://entertainment.timesonline.co.uk/tol/arts_and_entertainment/books/non-fiction/article6741878.ece]

and experience the stories we tell, but they should also be a primary source of those stories. The most memorable tales are the ones we can picture ourselves inside of. The most memorable characters are those who we can relate to and imagine walking in their shoes. So, organizations that tell relatable narratives will be better equipped to connect with their target audience. Telling stories about people like them is the most effective path to this outcome.

Your company is not the hero of the story. Too many businesses start by telling their history. They brag about their achievements and the credentials of their founders. But who cares? Your audience isn't interested in your revenue or stockholder value. They want to know how you can help them. They're interested in knowing why they should do business with you.

When you only focus on your organization, you fail to invite the audience into the narrative. They don't know what role they play. Or worse, they think you view them only as a way to boost the bottom line. No one wants to feel like a dollar sign on your sales sheet. Starting with a story about you reveals your business as being selfish and shortsighted.

Turn this around by making the audience the hero of your stories. Put them in the protagonist's seat by telling a story about someone like them—a person with issues and challenges they face in their life. Even if the story's character isn't exactly like them, they can relate to the specificity of the story. That automatically triggers them to craft a similar story in their minds.

Know Your Audience

Knowing your audience is simultaneously the most cliched and true element of business, marketing, and storytelling. This is an easy thing to say (which is why it's repeated ad nauseum), but it's another thing to practice. Some people even think they know their audience, but don't have the first clue.

Knowing your audience begins by understanding what the term even means. Audience is a problematically broad term. It could mean any number of things.

When Aerosmith does a concert, Steven Tyler knows who his audience is—it's the tens of thousands of people packed into the venue. When he yells at them, they cheer. When they finish a song, they applaud. The band gets immediate feedback on their performance. They can reach out and crowd surf on their audience. There is a visible interaction between performers and fans.

Businesses don't have that luxury. We don't always see or directly touch our potential customers. There's a distance and approximation involved. We're not rockstars and we don't have groupies—at least most of us. We rely on different methods for communicating with and getting feedback from our audience.

Our definition of an audience is different. In our case, our audience is current and potential customers, clients, supporters, donors, or anyone who might mutually benefit from doing business with our company. That's still broad, but it at least gives us guardrails to play within.

Doing the Research

Now that we better understand who fits into our audience, it's time to get to know them. But what information is helpful to have? Develop a more complete picture of your audience by learning:

- Their goals
- Their aspirations
- Their values
- Their pain points
- What confuses them
- What scares them
- What motivates them
- Where they live
- How they communicate
- How they spend their time
- How they spend their money

Where do you find this information? You can certainly find studies and data collected by the government or Pew Research. You could guess based on your personal experience. An even easier way to find out is just to ask your audience directly.

That could come in the form of formal surveys and interviews. Balance these out with more casual conversations with potential clients or current customers. Ask them about their experiences, both with your business and beyond. You can be honest and let them know what it's for. When you frame it as a way for you to help serve them better, they're more likely to help.

Create Fictional Personas

Collecting helpful information from your audience is worthless without a way to utilize it. Perhaps the best use for the details is building audience personas. These are fictional (but realistic) representations of your target group that gives you something to aim for.

Your business can have multiple personas, but fewer is better and there should only be one persona per audience segment. For example, High-end Harry for your company's more expensive products or Bargain Barbara for your more price-conscious consumer.

These personas take time to create and should be refined as you learn more about your audience. But they're an invaluable internal tool for your team, especially as you tell stories. As you create a story, pretend like you're doing it specifically for this individual.

When you remember that your audience is a collection of people (and not just data points), your storytelling is more human.

You're Not The Hero

If your business isn't the hero, what role do you play? (Hopefully, not the villain.) What's the point of telling stories at your business if they don't ultimately benefit you? There's another way to position your company in a way that builds trust and leads people toward doing business with you.

Position yourself as the Story Guide.

Searching for a Story

The commercial begins with a blinking computer cursor. With classical music playing in the background, an unknown person types in their first search: "study abroad paris france." Over the next 60 seconds, our unseen protagonist makes a dozen searches, including "impress a french girl," "long-distance relationship advice," and culminating with "how to assemble a crib." These small, everyday queries fit together to tell a heartwarming story.

Appropriately entitled 'Parisian Love,' this commercial was also the first television ad for the internet search giant Google. The spot ran during the 2010 Super Bowl, and was so well received that it inspired several similar ads in later years, which Google affectionately calls their 'Search Stories.'

"The ads reflect our goal to build products that help people in their daily lives, in both big and small ways," said Google CMO Lorraine Twohill. "[They are] simple love stories told through the lens of our products."[9]

Google was famously started as a research project in 1998 by two Stanford Ph.D. students: Larry Page and Sergey Brin. Other search engines existed at the time—Yahoo, Lycos, or AltaVista. But they weren't as effective at finding what users were looking for online.

With the internet exploding in size, Page and Brin realized the need to build a better (computer) mousetrap. Their mission was "to organize the world's information and make it universally accessible and useful."

---

9   Google and the Super Bowl: Here to help, by Lorraine Twohill, January 28, 2020 [https://www.blog.google/products/assistant/google-super-bowl-here-to-help]

The original name of their site was 'Backrub,' a reference to their focus on backlinks, which are links from another website back to yours. From Google's perspective, the more backlinks, the better. That's because each subsequent link is like a vote of confidence in your online content. Better quality sites will be linked more often—at least that's the theory.

This breakthrough in online search is what set Google apart from the other search engines. They desired to bring more relevant search results to users by cross-indexing the entire internet.

Another point of differentiation was their home page, which to this day is minimalist and simple. Rather than selling dozens of banner ads on their site to earn money, they decided to put text-only ads within the searches themselves. This led to a cleaner search experience for the individual user and delivered them ads that were more relevant to what they searched for.

Speaking of ads, it took twelve years between when the company was officially founded and when they launched that Super Bowl ad. By that time, Google had become a household name—not just as a company, but as the shorthand for searching anything online. You don't Yahoo or Bing something, you Google it.

The search giant could have easily touted their brand recognition or secret algorithm or countless other products (like Gmail or Google Maps) in the commercial—but they distinctly chose to go another direction. They chose to tell a story, not about themselves, but about the people who use their service in their everyday lives.

With ubiquitous brands like Google or Coke or Nike, people don't need to hear about the history or the features of the company—we're already abundantly familiar with them.

Instead, it's far better to share the smaller moments of how they can enhance our lives. That's exactly what Google did with 'Parisian Love.'

Google wasn't the hero of that story; it was the faceless protagonist who went to Paris and fell in love with a French girl. By leaving the character anonymous, Google allowed the viewer to fit themselves into the protagonist's point of view. After all, we use Google all of the time—so why not use its information to travel to another country, learn another language, or get married?

Google set itself apart from other early search engines by establishing itself as our guide to the world-wide web's intricate network of websites and information. They reinforced that idea by showing how they can guide us through the world outside of the internet. They told a story about how they can lead us through any challenge with just the right search.

Even if you see big technology companies as oppressive Big Brother, that concept of setting your business as the guide to your audience's story is a key component of earning their trust.

Your Organization as The Guide

Once you've infected your audience with a story, that's only half of the journey. How your audience experiences this story and what they choose to do with it afterward influences how you continue to share stories at your organization. Because when you do this right, it should build a nearly-perpetual flow of story sharing and creation.

All stories have characters, but not all characters are created equally. Most of our attention is focused on the struggle of good vs. evil embodied by the protagonist and antagonist. But we often overlook the importance of the guide.

- Gandalf in *Lord of the Rings.*
- Dumbledore in *Harry Potter.*
- Obi-Wan Kenobi and Yoda in *Star Wars.*
- Morpheus in *The Matrix.*
- Mr. Miyagi in *The Karate Kid.*
- Aslan in *The Lion, The Witch, and the Wardrobe.*
- Rafiki in *The Lion King.*

These characters all guide (appropriately enough) the protagonist along their journey. They provide expertise and wisdom. Where the hero is weak and lost, the guide is strong and confident. The main character needs this guidance to reach their full potential.

Guides are trusted and competent. They're wise and experienced. The guide wants the main character to succeed in their quest. Even better, the guide is willing to assist along the way. **By establishing yourself as a guide, you position your business to earn your customers' trust and help make their lives better.**

Donald Miller started his career as a best-selling author of books like *Blue Like Jazz* and *A Million Miles in a Thousand Years.* These were both introspective memoirs about spirituality and self-discovery. These books helped Miller realize the power of story and how he could help others harness that same power.

Miller founded a business (called StoryBrand) around that idea, and his book *Building a Story Brand* walks business leaders through telling more meaningful stories. Many of the concepts in this book come from the StoryBrand framework. In a meta way, Miller went from being the hero of his story—as the protagonist and narrator of each of his early books—to the wise-old guide. Now his goal is to help others discover their own story. He uses his experience and knowledge to lead businesses.

The stories you tell—from case studies, online reviews, testimonials, and more—are what earn you credibility as the guide. These stories build a narrative that invites the audience to participate. To make your business as wise as Gandalf and as trusted as Aslan, you must do two things: identify your story goals and build a story team.

Identify Your Story Goals

Story is the ultimate organizational buzzword, especially within marketing. It takes no effort to pepper the term 'story' into your vocabulary and think you've made a monumental change within your company. But why are you bothering with story sharing in the first place? What are you trying to accomplish?

If it's to try to make yourself feel better or to impress your boss, then you likely don't need to put in much work. The illusion of storytelling is relatively easy to summon. But if you're genuinely attempting to grow your business by building customer loyalty through real stories, that's a different animal—one that requires significantly more strategy and time.

For our purposes, we'll assume that you're trying to muster a real effort. We'll assume that you care about using stories for the right reasons. But what are those reasons? What outcomes are you after?

For some businesses, that could be establishing your brand and growing awareness among potential customers. For other companies, it might be rehabbing your image and trying to pivot your existing brand in a new direction. Your goal could be to educate an audience on why they need your product. Or maybe even an effort to build customer loyalty with your existing clients.

Whatever the story goal your business is aiming for, this should be the focal point of your story strategy. When you have a clear end in mind, you're more likely to hit it. And when you have a definite target, you'll be more intentional about telling the right stories.

Schedule a brainstorming meeting to come up with possible story goals and narrow down the right one for your organization. You might have several purposes in mind, but make an effort to prioritize your top goal. Be decisive and specific with what you're trying to accomplish.

But who gets invited to this story goal party? Who is aboard the train that's going to take you to this goal? Those segue questions lead us to your second step: building a story team.

Build your Story Team

Organizational story sharing never happens alone. We tell ourselves stories all the time—about our accomplishments, about how we look, about the people around us. Those internal stories can (even unconsciously) shape who we are and how we act. But they're never as influential or meaningful until we share them with other people.

The same is true for the process of gathering and sharing stories in our business. You may feel like the lone flag bearer for your company's story, but you shouldn't be. Seriously, going at it by yourself is lonely and ineffective. **You get more done by empowering others to participate in the Story Cycle.** Here are a few key roles that you can add to your story team.

- **Listener**: there are stories out there, but you need help to find them. We'll uncover more of what makes a good story listener in the chapter on Capturing the story.

- **Craftsman**: a story's raw materials need to be shaped to be effective. We'll dive more into what it takes to be a story craftsman in the Crafting the story chapter.

- **Sharer**: it's one thing to tell a story, but another to spread it like a disease (in a good way!). Let's uncover more about the story sharers in the Communicate the story chapter.

Story team—assemble!

Starting with the Guide

Because the Story Cycle is a cycle (plot twist!), there's no real beginning or end. Ideally, it's perpetual. You can theoretically start at any point in the process. But that doesn't work so well for a book, so we have to begin somewhere.

It helps to begin at the top of the guide half of the Cycle for simplicity. That's where most storytellers begin—the trouble is that's also where they stop. We'll follow through the Cycle by looking at the audience half. And your business can't know what stories to tell without first listening.

In Summary

- Businesses tell true stories that involve real people. These stories present you with the opportunity to invite your audience into the narrative.

- Your brand is not the hero of your story. That honor falls to your audience.

- This requires knowing your audience and keeping them as your stories' focus.

- If your business isn't the hero, then what role do you play? Effective brands act as a guide that helps their audience get what they need.

- To become the guide, you need to know your story goals and assemble a storytelling team to do the work.

PART 2

YOUR ORGANIZATION AS THE STORYTELLING GUIDE

"A good storyteller doesn't just tell
a better story, though.
He invites other people into the story with him,
giving them a better story, too."
—Donald Miller,
A Million Miles in a Thousand Years

CHAPTER 4

CAPTURE THE STORY

Big Idea: Before you can tell great stories, you must listen for them.

Forming the Corps

When Dave Isay was 22, he learned that his father was gay. As part of a close family, this was shocking news to Dave. His father's revelation was a challenging pill to swallow. Through their conversations, Isay's father told him about the Stonewall Riots, which was the beginning of the modern gay rights movement in 1969.

Isay had just begun a career in radio and had the idea to record the stories of those involved with the Riots. Microphone and tape recorder in hand, Isay began having conversations with people he otherwise might never have had the opportunity to. And in so doing, told the stories behind the Stonewall Riots to a national audience for the first time.

Over the next 15 years, Isay continued to create more

radio documentaries. He discovered that the very nature of allowing someone to tell their story allowed them to feel like they were being seen. So many regular people live on the margins of society and often don't feel like they're truly allowed to exist. Having their stories heard and shared changed that.

Inspired by this power, Isay wanted to spread this concept. He wanted to remove the limitations on the power of stories from just the documentaries he was able to share on the radio. He hoped to scale the light that was being shone on regular stories.

Isay was a shy kid who appreciated solitude, but he also enjoyed spending time around older people and listening to their stories. One dinner, he was with his grandparents and a few other relatives. They spent the evening going around the dinner table, sharing stories. Dave found an old tape recorder and began capturing those yarns. Despite his youth and inexperience, Isay could tell his relatives appreciated being listened to.

Over the years, those relatives passed away. Every time he visited his grandparents' house, Dave looked for that recorder where he'd captured their stories. But he couldn't find it. He regretted not being able to listen back to their voices and the tales they told. So, he resolved to help others capture the meaningful stories in their lives.

In 2003, Dave Isay set up a recording booth in Grand Central Station in Manhattan—one of the busiest places in the world, in a city where it's easy to feel invisible and unheard. The recording studio was an invitation for anyone to have an intimate and personal conversation with another human being.

Capture the Story

The concept was simple.

- Two strangers stepped into the booth.
- They spent an hour taking turns asking and answering questions.
- The entire conversation was recorded.
- Both participants got a copy of the recording; another was archived.

That's how StoryCorps was born.

From the first booth in Grand Central, the organization set up two more mobile booths outside of the Library of Congress in Washington D.C. By 2007, the organization released a book called *Listening Is an Act of Love* that shared the story behind the stories. The book became a New York Times bestseller. That same year, StoryCorps was awarded an institutional Peabody Award.

The next few years saw more stories collected and more books published. StoryCorps launched initiatives to recognize the stories of unheard communities: African Americans, the LGBTQ+ community, students and teachers, and those impacted by incarceration.

Today, the StoryCorps mission is "to preserve and share humanity's stories in order to build connections between people and create a more just and compassionate world." Isay believes together we can create an archive of the wisdom of humanity.

Since those beginnings, StoryCorps has captured over 500,000 individual stories, making it the largest archive of collected audio stories in the world.

"You can find the most amazing stories from regular people. All you have to do is ask them about their lives and listen," said Isay. "We can learn so much about the people around us, even about the people we already know, just by taking the time to have a conversation. If you pay a little attention, you'll find wisdom and poetry in their words."[10]

Nearly a decade after founding StoryCorps, Dave Isay's dad had become a psychiatrist and successful gay-rights activist. Despite being in good health, he was diagnosed with cancer and passed away suddenly on June 28, 2012. That day was the anniversary of the Stonewall Riots.

On the day his father died, Isay listened to the recording of their conversation—the recording that indirectly inspired the recordings of so many other stories. Losing his father was no doubt sad. But that loss was tempered with a lasting testament to his legacy.

Story Listening

Stories are everywhere. Every person is full of stories. The world is full of people, so it's saturated by the stories we have to tell. If stories are living things, we humans are the ones who give birth to them. We're also the ones who continue to give them life.

We keep stories alive by encountering them, absorbing them, and passing them along. Through listening to another person's story, we give that narrative another mind to inhabit. That's how stories spread. That's how they achieve a wider

---

10 An Introduction to StoryCorps from our Founder, Dave Isay (Sept 15, 2015)

reach than just the individual or group who experienced the story first-hand.

As Dave Isay and StoryCorps demonstrate, listening to another person's stories shows them respect and dignity. **You see and treat others differently when you've heard their personal narrative.** It helps you better understand them. Story Listening is one of the most powerful tools we have to serve others.

As a society, we're often overly focused on Story Telling. That's the buzzword we freely toss around. We understandably want to tell our stories. However, we often overlook the power of listening to the stories of others. Just like Story Telling, Story Listening is a skill that is crafted and improved over time. It comes more naturally to some, but it always takes time and practice.

Organizations have stories because organizations are full of people. The history of a company is the collective stories of the people who came together to form that group. If you're a business leader hoping to tell your organization's story, you must listen to the stories of those around you.

That doesn't just mean the founders or executives of your organization. It's tempting to tell our own stories. But that's an incomplete and self-serving purpose. Your company's story is better served by amplifying the voices of your employees, your clients, your community, your volunteers, your vendors, and anyone else you encounter.

By telling the stories of your people, you share a message that invites in others just like them.

Human Stories

Brandon Stanton lost his finance job in Chicago in 2010. He took the opportunity to move to New York City and start a career in photography. At the time, he was broke. He'd never been to New York before and didn't know anyone there. Plus, he only had six months of photography experience.

What could go wrong?

In the same city that gave birth to StoryCorps just a few years earlier, Stanton was surrounded by stories. He knew there were few other places on earth to find a wider diversity and variety of people and stories than NYC.

Stanton started a Facebook page to share his photos. His goal was to collect 10,000 portraits of New Yorkers and plot them on a virtual map of the city. He worked daily snapping pictures and posting them online. The photos got some attention but were largely lost in the sea of social media.

Things changed when Stanton started asking his subjects a few questions as he took their photos. He included their first-person testimonials as photo captions. These stories added to the pictures' impact. The narrative captions provided depth and context behind each image.

"I was already going through the effort to approach a stranger and get them to let me take their photo. It was only a small step from that to speaking with this person, and learning about their lives, learning about their stories."[11]

It might seem unbelievable that strangers would be willing to share their secrets with some dude with a camera. But Stanton found that his anonymity allowed them to open

11 Meet the Creator Behind the Photo Blog Humans of New York (ABC News, Oct 13, 2015)

up to him. People are more willing to be open and honest than we'd realize—especially when they know that the guy with the camera might just share that story with someone else.

Stanton named his collection of online stories Humans of New York (HONY).

"Humans of New York is an amazing story," said Stanton in a Huffington Post article. "Without social media, I'd probably just be a quirky, amateur photographer with a hard drive full of photos... I may have even quit by now. Instead, I've discovered a daily audience of nearly a million people."

In the decade since it started, HONY has exploded in popularity and reach. The social media following alone regularly reaches millions of people with each post. Stanton has published several book compilations of these stories. More than that, it's begun expanding outside of New York.

After the Boston Marathon bombing, Stanton began collecting stories around Boston. In 2014, he partnered with the United Nations on a 50-day World Tour—visiting twelve countries around the world. He's been to Iran and Pakistan to share stories and raise awareness of issues happening around the globe.

During COVID-19, Humans of New York opened up to outside submissions for the first time. The goal was to share inspirational and uplifting stories to give people hope during the crisis.

The organization has also inspired other photographers and storytellers to follow a similar format. Dozens of other "Humans Of" blogs and social media accounts have sprung up around the internet: including Humans of Bombay, Rome, Sydney, and Amsterdam. Although none are as well-known as the original, they're following in the same footsteps and weaving together a larger tapestry of human-based story listening.

Because humans, of New York or otherwise, all have stories worth listening to.

Hunting vs Gathering For Stories

Listening to people's stories should always be an active occupation. It's a matter of respect and professionalism to pay attention to your subject.

- Focus on what they're saying.
- Take written notes.
- Record the story in either audio or video.
- Go back and review their story later.

That's when you're listening *to* a story. However, there are two different methods of listening *for* new stories within your organization: either actively or passively. And the best Story Telling organizations practice a fair measure of both.

Humans of New York actively collect stories, which can be called **Story Hunting**. Brandon Stanton and his team intentionally approach people on the street, request to take their photos, and then ask the subjects direct questions about themselves. That's an active approach with the organization taking the initiative to collect a story from an otherwise passive subject.

StoryCorps typically takes a more passive approach to story collection. They set up sound booths and leave them open for people to volunteer to enter a story conversation with another person. In contrast to Story Hunting, we call this process **Story Gathering**. They're simply setting up a net to collect stories as they pass by. The impetus is on the people who want their stories heard.

Your organization can implement both aspects of Story Listening: both Hunting and Gathering.

- Set up story collection forms on your website.
- Add the occasional call for interesting stories on your social media channels.
- Invite people to reply with their stories in your email newsletter.
- Listen out for people volunteering their stories in casual conversations.

These are ways of signaling to your audience that you're open to hearing from them. However, they'll need to be the ones to take action. These are the nets that your organization sets out in the wild to passively filter occasional stories wandering by.

On occasion, your company might want to take a more active approach to hunting for stories within your community. Ask your team or advisors if they've heard any meaningful stories from customers. Approach specific people with a plan of action for an interview. This takes more planning and intentionality (not to mention just a bit of courage), but you're more likely to find good stories than just by waiting for them to come to you.

Hunting and gathering are two distinctly different but equally valuable approaches to collecting effective stories within your organization.

Missing Stories

There will always be stories within your organization that you miss. There's no potential way you capture and share them all. That shouldn't be your goal. Your goal should be to listen for the right stories and be prepared to capture them as you encounter them.

At the risk of sounding obvious, **you can't tell the stories you don't hear.** You also can't share the stories that you don't remember or don't have any details for. Missing a story means missing the opportunity to share it with others and keep the story alive. Failing to capture the right information means failing to tell the story properly.

As living things, **stories survive when they're cared for and passed along.** Missing a story breaks the Story Cycle. Neglecting to record a story breaks the Story Cycle. Breaking the Story Cycle eliminates the opportunity for that story to inspire others. Your goal is to capture the right stories that could give birth to even more stories.

There are three ways you might miss a story within your organization: not listening, not recording, and not archiving.

Not Listening

It should be clear by now that Story Listening is a crucial first step before you're able to tell stories. You must take the time to hunt and gather before you're able to share the goods with others.

There are plenty of reasons why an organizational leader might not listen for stories. Perhaps they don't know how, yet. Maybe they don't yet grasp its importance. The most common excuse is a lack of time or resources. Properly listening for stories requires intentionally carving out a margin to sit with others and hear their stories.

There are no shortcuts to effective organizational storytelling. If you want to do Story Telling correctly, you must first invest your time into Story Listening.

Not Recording

Once you take the time to listen, you'll start to encounter stories from your audience—stories of heartache, stories of triumph, and stories that are so funny that you do a spit take. If they're interesting enough, you'll be enraptured by the narrative.

Remember: you're not the only one who should hear this story. You need to capture what they're telling to share it again on their behalf. As you listen, record what they're saying. Take photos or videos. Write notes. These are the raw elements you'll use to craft into a bigger story later.

What would Humans of New York be without all of those beautiful photos? What would StoryCorps be without those thousands of recorded conversations? Those organizations are only impactful because they understand the importance of recording the stories they hear.

If you're still unclear on how to record stories, don't worry. In the next section, we'll look through some specifics on how to record elements for the most impact.

Not Archiving

It's not enough to take a bunch of notes or photos from a conversation and call it a day. Imagine if StoryCorps had to sift through half a million audio recordings to find a single story. Or if Humans of New York had no system for the tens of thousands of photos they've taken.

To properly scale storytelling at your organization, you need some organizational structure to store these raw ingredients.

Notes, audio recordings, and video clips will be lost or forgotten if you're not careful. Editing elements of a story would take a frustratingly long time with no way to search or sort files. That's why the next section also has an idea for how to organize your recordings into a useful archive.

How to Story Listen

Stories are the native language of human beings. There's a reason why StoryCorps and Humans of New York have become so popular. Not just because they're based around storytelling. But because they're tapping into the power of everyday stories. They've found a way to capture and elevate humanity with the content they share.

They both exhibit basic lessons all of us can learn to better Story Listen within our organizations.

Form a Personal Connection

Dave Isay began by listening to the stories of his family. Brandon Stanton started taking photos of strangers. But both made their subjects feel safe and comfortable by listening.

They focused on how the act of listening could help the other person feel seen through sharing their story. This is a skill that takes time to develop, but can only be done through practice and patience.

Don't overlook the importance of earning the right to tell

someone else's story. These narratives can be deeply personal and emotionally charged. Being allowed to share these stories on a public level takes trust. Building these relationships takes time. Don't take that trust lightly.

Always Be Prepared

Before I attended journalism school, my dad (also a journalist) gave me two gifts: a box full of reporter notepads and a digital audio recorder. These were the tools of the trade that I was setting off to learn, and those tools have come in handy.

After my four years in college, I'd filled up those notebooks with scribbles from newspaper interviews and ideas for articles to write. I'd also worn down the record button on that audio recorder from countless interviews. Both tools fit easily into my back pocket and went nearly everywhere that I did.

A good journalist (or storyteller) always carries a pen and paper with them. Because **stories are everywhere and you'll never know when you'll bump into a good one.**

Smartphones have combined the features of a camera, recorder, and notepad into one device. And you'd be hard-pressed to find someone who *isn't* carrying a phone at all times. Practice using your phone to collect stories—whether that's through photos, video, audio, or text notes.

StoryCorps captures their stories in an audio format. They use microphones, sound booths, and people's voices. Humans of New York shares stories through photographs and photo captions. They use cameras and human faces to tell stories. Regardless of the medium you use, it's crucial to always be prepared with a means of capturing stories as they appear.

Archive the Stories

As you collect elements of stories, you need to save them somewhere. An archive ensures that they'll be protected and accessible when you need them. StoryCorps houses their archive at the American Folklife Center at the Library of Congress in Washington, D.C. Humans of New York publishes their stories more publicly—sharing them on a range of social media channels.

Not all of your stories will be shareable, at least not immediately. It's better to record those story pieces and create a place where they can be found and assembled later. Think of this as your **Storytelling Library**. Your Storytelling Library is a safe place where you can review the stories you need during specific campaigns or marketing materials.

This could be a collection of audio sound bites, video clips, photos, text quotes, or all of the above. Make sure it's a place your entire team can easily access and search. For that reason, internal or cloud-based servers are good options for creating your Storytelling Library.

Once you've listened, recorded, and saved the elements of your story, you're ready for the next step in the Story Cycle. You're ready to assemble and edit these pieces into a well-crafted story.

In Summary

- Every organization has stories to tell because they're involved with people. To find those stories, you need to practice listening for them.

- Telling the stories of your people sends an inviting message to others like them. However, listening for stories is an investment that requires both patience and practice.

- Story Listening requires a few different techniques—both actively hunting for stories and passively gathering them from your audience.

- You'll miss the best stories if you aren't listening, not properly recording them, or failing to archive them in a way that can be used for later.

- Listening to your audience requires forming a personal connection, constantly being ready to record a story, and creating an organizational Story Library.

CHAPTER 5

CRAFT THE STORY

Big Idea: You can't share a story in its raw form; you must polish it first.

May the Story Be With You

Not that long ago, in a dark screening room not that far away, a scrappy young director named George Lucas hosted a viewing party for the rough cut of his new film. The invite list was short but included other budding directors—among them two guys named Steven Spielberg and Brian DePalma.

The movie they saw is now as well-known as those legendary film figures—*Star Wars: A New Hope*.

Except that the movie they watched that day wasn't *Star Wars*—at least, not yet. It was a poor excuse for a forerunner of the now-classic space adventure. The then 33-year-old Lucas bore most of the creative weight of the film, including directing and screenwriting. And at that stage in his career, Lucas hadn't yet crafted his signature storytelling style.

By all accounts, the rough-cut Spielberg, DePalma, and others sneak peeked was objectively bad. DePalma, who by that time had already directed *Carrie* and would go on to create such cinematic masterpieces as *Scarface, The Untouchables,* and *Mission: Impossible,* remarked that the movie didn't make any sense.

As directors, they understood there would be issues with a rough cut. At the early stage, they could look past the unfinished audio, inserted stock photos, and missing special effects. But the issues ran much deeper than that. What Lucas' confidants witnessed that day was a problem with the story.

The narrative, order of scenes, and film's pacing were miserable. Thankfully, the collected directors understood enough to see the glimmer of promise amongst the chaos. There was still hope to save the nascent film—which was appropriate given its name. So, with his friend's suggestions in hand, Lucas turned to his editors.

Paul Hirsch, Richard Chew, and Marcia Lucas comprised the film editing team that would spend countless hours reworking the story. They took the raw materials the director had given them and completely revitalized it into a comprehensive story.

Hirsch recounted how he began the film editing process in his memoir *A Long Time Ago in a Cutting Room Far, Far Away*:

"I started reshuffling some of the shots, shortening them, tightening the cuts to the action. A rhythm started to develop . . . When I was done, the sequence was a minute shorter, a bit over three minutes instead of four, but there was more in it."[12]

---

12 *A Long Time Ago in a Cutting Room Far, Far Away*, Paul Hirsch, pages 192

Scraps of film began to pile up on the cutting room floor. But with every splice, the story got tighter and clearer. By taking the wrong pieces away, the editors made the story stronger. Only by breaking down the narrative and building it back up could the editing team form the universe a long time ago and far, far away that we know and love today.

For their work, the *Star Wars* editing team won an Academy Award for Best Film Editing. They pieced together a story that has captured the hearts and minds of millions. And not just for one film—*A New Hope's* success launched a series of films, TV shows, and an entire land at Disney World.

By knowing what elements to keep and which to cut, these editors saved *Star Wars*. They also give us a prime example of the power of properly crafting a story.

Assembling Stories

There are lots of varying definitions for the word 'draft.' It can mean to be selected by a sports team or refer to a closed current of air. But there's one specific definition of a draft that we're focused on for the Story Cycle.

That definition of draft refers to "a preliminary sketch, outline, or version." Because every story starts with a first draft. **Every story begins somewhere, and that somewhere is always objectively worse than the final version.** That's why they call it a rough draft.

In her book, *Bird by Bird*, writer Anne Lamont refers to these as "crappy first drafts." (Except she doesn't use the word "crappy.")

"All good writers write them. This is how they end up with good second drafts and terrific third drafts . . . The first draft is the child's draft, where you let it all pour out and then let it romp all over the place, knowing that no one is going to see it and that you can shape it later."[13]

The first time you put together your organization's story, it's not going to be perfect—far from it. That's the point. If you wait until it's just right, you'll constantly be waiting. Your goal should be to get started and make the content better through repetition.

Building your story goes far beyond just correcting grammatical mistakes (although that's important, too). **Crafting a story is about discovering the core of your story and polishing that until it shines.** That process starts with gathering the elements of your story and assembling them in the best narrative pattern.

The goal of Story Listening is to capture a story in its raw form. Collect all of the emotional and human thoughts and ideas of your subject. Get them down on paper or video and add them to your growing Story Library. But realize that these stories in their raw form aren't ready to be shared with your audience. They must be edited first.

Story Crafting means deciding what details are right for the audience. It means collecting multiple stories from a variety of people and perspectives and stitching them together into a single, cohesive narrative. It means digging deep for the elements that transform one person's amusing anecdote into a true, world-changing story.

It's worth referencing George Lucas' Star Wars universe

---

13   *Bird by Bird,* Anne Lamott, pgs 21-22

again. *A New Hope* was the first Star Wars film produced, but not the first chronologically in the story. Lucas famously began by telling the middle of the story and only years later (controversially) did he share the story's beginning. This was an intentional creative decision. **The chronology and order of your narrative matter.**

Even after releasing the films, Lucas wasn't done editing. LucasFilms eventually released a special, remastered edition of the original *Star Wars* trilogy in the 1990s. The new editions primarily focused on improved special effects, but they also introduced new scenes into the movies. George Lucas continued to tinker with the narrative and try new ways to make it better.

A story is a living thing. **You can continue to edit and craft the story even as you tell it.**

How to Assemble Stories

Start by assembling your story. Pull together the pieces you collected during the first phase of the Story Cycle. Put them in an order that makes sense. Like George Lucas trying to reorganize the jumbled pieces in *Star Wars*, you must form order out of the chaos.

Your goal is to create a seamless and fluid experience for your audience. Watch out for speed bumps that jar them loose or be a distraction from your message. Pay attention to transitions—poor transitions leave your audience behind. Build tension towards a meaningful resolution.

Organizational stories contain different details that fit together like blocks to create a final narrative. Assembling a story draft is like stringing those individual pieces together for the best sequence. Think of them like notes in a song or words in a sentence—matter orders. (Or maybe the other way around.)

Decide on the Details

Gather the details from the story you captured in the first phase of the Story Cycle. Place them in front of you—whether that's on sticky notes or in a Word document. This gives you the perspective to get them all in the right order. The goal is to find a flow that gets your point across.

As you assemble your story draft, remember to look for the four, story elements we covered earlier—context, character, conflict, and change. Ensure all four elements are represented and are balanced appropriately. Some stories rely more heavily on one or two of these elements, which is fine. But don't lean on them to the detriment of the other elements.

Understanding how conflict, change, character, and context work together will help you find the right order for your story. But even when you have the right pieces, your story isn't fully crafted. Even a well-organized story still needs some polishing. We'll get to that soon.

Decide on the Scope

What is the size of the story you're going to tell?

- How long will your speech be?
- How many words should the blog-post run?
- What will the runtime of your video be?
- How many images should you include in your photo album?

Setting the scope of your story helps you determine the pacing and level of detail. The scope will depend on your context—especially your audience and the platform you're using. Many platforms have natural limitations—like a character count on Twitter or the duration of a 30-second TV ad. But your audience's attention span is another limitation. For example, if you're telling a story to a bunch of teenagers in a high school gym, you better grab their attention quickly and don't try to hold on for too long.

Organize into a Narrative

Once you have the details and the scope, it's time to build a cohesive narrative. It's like assembling the tracks and cars in a train. Get the order right, connect everything together, and ensure that it's heading in the proper direction.

There's a term that filmmakers like George Lucas would be familiar with: a storyboard. This could take the form of note cards on a bulletin board, or digital software. Either way, the point is to organize your story with a visual representation of each scene or section.

Storyboards are vital to films because of the need to get things in the right order. "A video without a storyboard is like a house without a foundation," said marketing advisor and entrepreneur, Han-Gwon Lung. Even if you're creating a video, you can still use a similar tool to arrange your ideas.

Pay close attention to the transitions between sections of your story. Is the jump from ideas or sections smooth, or rough? Do they make sense and build on one another? Or do they leave your audience lost? Your goal is to ensure that the ride is turbulence-free from start to finish.

Speaking of transitions, let's segue into our next section with an example that highlights the importance of a smooth narrative. It's a story that started with a bumpy beginning but has since grown into a widely beloved example of innovative storytelling.

To Stories and Beyond

Their dream was to create the first-ever computer-animated film.

But the Pixar Animation Studios existed for several years before coming anywhere close to this dream. Pixar was born as the special effects division of LucasFilms, the studio that created *Star Wars*. To pay for his divorce, George Lucas sold Pixar to a guy named Steve Jobs, who'd recently been forced out of a little company he'd founded, called Apple.

With Jobs' funding, Pixar eventually shifted from a struggling software development company to fully focusing on computer animation. The team produced a few short films and TV commercials that showed promise. They were getting closer to fulfilling their dream.

It would come much closer when the little-studio-that-could signed a three-picture deal with Disney, the animation giant Pixar snatched most of its talent from. Under the deal, Disney would provide distribution, funding, and promotion.

All Pixar had to do was make the movie. But first, they needed an idea.

Director John Lasseter, a former Disney animator, came up with the concept for a movie told from the perspective of a group of toys. They'd already produced a short film called *Tin Toy* several years earlier, so the idea seemed promising. The problem was the story.

Woody the cowboy featured prominently in the first drafts of *Toy Story*, but he was much different from the version audiences would eventually see on screen. Based on the feedback from Disney executives, they made Woody darker and edgier. He was jealous of Buzz Lightyear and violently tossed him out a window. He bossed around the other toys and called them names.

According to Pixar founder Ed Catmull, this version of Woody was "wholly unappealing." The animated cowboy had "become a jerk."[14] Rather than the protagonist of the film, Woody was more like the villain. And this unlikeable protagonist was spoiling the rest of *Toy Story*.

One of the people brought on to help in this process of fixing the story was "script doctor" Joss Whedon. The up-and-coming screenwriter had already helped with plot issues in blockbuster films, including *Speed*. When Whedon got ahold of the story, he agreed with Catmull's criticism:

> "[T]he movie was unwatchable. The story had lost the heart that Tin Toy had; the leads, Woody the cowboy and Buzz Lightyear the astronaut, were sarcastic and unlikeable—not exactly ideal heroes for a children's movie."[15]

Even the Disney executives agreed with the assessment, shutting production down on the film until a better storyline could be crafted. It was up to the Pixar team to rewrite the script and learn to "trust their own storytelling instincts."

---

14   *Creativity Inc,* Ed Catmull page 57

15   *Joss Wheden: The Biography,* Amy Pascale (2014)

To add to the pressure, a lot was riding on getting the movie right. Jobs had scheduled Pixar's IPO for a few days after the film's eventual release. If the movie did well, it would catapult the animation studio into success. A blockbuster hit would provide enough funding to make more animated films. However, if *Toy Story* was a flop, it could potentially bankrupt Pixar.

As you can guess, the team sorted out the issues with *Toy Story* and released the first full-length animated feature film to critical and popular success in 1995. Woody was more likable and his relationship with Buzz Lightyear became the emotional core of the film. Pixar had discovered a story that would amaze audiences as much as their animation technology.

Not only did this help to launch Pixar into early fame, but it also helped them learn a valuable lesson: "Story is King." As Catmull describes it in his memoir, *Creativity, Inc.*:

"We would let nothing—not the technology, not the merchandising possibilities—get in the way of our story. We took pride in the fact that the reviewers talked mainly about the way *Toy Story* made them feel and not about the computer wizardry that enabled us to get it up on the screen. We believed that this was the direct result of our always keeping story as our guiding light."[16]

It's apparent to anyone who has watched any of Pixar's subsequent films that they've kept this principle alive and

16   *Creativity Inc.*, Ed Catmull, page 66 (2014)

well. The storytellers at Pixar have used this principle as the filter for how they polish and shape the stories they tell.

The lessons they learned from creating *Toy Story* demonstrate that editing finer details are critical to enjoying storytelling success.

Assembling vs. Editing

Every story needs to be assembled, but they also need to be edited. These are two distinct processes and need to be intentionally separated. Don't try to alternate between the two simultaneously. They take different parts of your brain. Trying to do both at once is like trying to simultaneously run and swim.

Once you've connected the story fragments into a cohesive narrative, it's time to edit that into a well-polished story. More than grammatical errors in a written story or errant frames in a video, **editing is about polishing the story into a finished product.** The raw materials you've assembled are rough. Editing smooths out the rough edges and makes them more appealing to the audience.

Assembling is the heavy lifting—it's moving the larger pieces in place so that there is a logical move from one idea to the next. Editing is paying attention to the smaller details and removing the distractions that might prevent your audience from flowing through the narrative.

- Assembling is a jackhammer.
  Editing is a hand chisel.
- Assembling is a paint roller.
  Editing is a fine paintbrush.

- Assembling is the big picture.
  Editing is the small details.

They're both needed but are handled differently. They require a different mindset and toolset. It helps to put them in a specific order—start with the big picture before settling on the details.

There's an anecdote about a legendary copywriter named David Ogilvy about the time he encountered a homeless man. The beggar held out a sign that read: "I'm blind, please help." Unfortunately, the sign wasn't drawing any sympathy. His donation cup was empty.

Rather than walking by, Ogilvy offered to help. According to legend, the copywriter took the sign from the homeless man and scribbled a few changes. He handed the sign back to the beggar with the promise that the new message would generate more donations.

A day later, Ogilvy revisited the homeless man, whose cup was now overflowing with spare change. In his hands, the beggar held the cardboard sign with Ovilvy's new narrative.

The sign read: "It is spring and I am blind."

Through editing, Ogilvy had changed the homeless man's sign from a predictable plea that we've (regrettably) all heard before into a story. It evokes a vision (pardon the pun) of happy spring days and contrasts that with the poor man's inability to enjoy the same experience. This emotional tension made the man's situation personal and compelled people into a more generous action.

That's the power of editing—the right words make all the difference.

Unpolished Stories

Raw Stories

Stories that haven't been edited aren't effective. The raw details of a story don't have the same impact as one that's been polished by a professional storyteller. Serving up a raw story would be like serving raw meat or unbaked bread. It's just not palatable. Like different foods, different stories require different levels of cooking or spices to make them edible and enjoyable. They require patience and taste-testing your story along the way to know when it's ready to be shared with others.

Unedited stories break the Story Cycle because they decrease the chances of the story resonating with the audience.

- An ineffective story isn't likely to inspire any additional stories.

- Boring stories overburdened with confusing or irrelevant details are quickly forgotten.

- Unprofessional stories that are full of mistakes or irrelevant details cause people to doubt your credibility.

Editing and assembling a narrative takes time and effort. But it's a worthwhile investment because it keeps the Story Cycle turning. These steps are like mixing the ingredients and cooking them at the right time and temperature. You're preparing something specifically for your dinner guests. And you don't want to give them food poisoning.

Overly Simplistic Stories

While you don't want to serve stories to people raw, you also don't want to dumb them down to the point where they become too simple or even untrue. It might be tempting to sidestep an uncomfortable truth or fail to mention a conflict of interest, but that's doing both your audience and your brand a disservice.

In his book *21 Lessons for the 21st Century*, historian Yuval Noah Harari had this to say about stories:

> "Homo sapiens is a storytelling animal that thinks in stories rather than in numbers or graphs, and believes that the universe itself works like a story, replete with heroes and villains, conflicts and resolutions, climaxes and happy endings. When we look for the meaning of life, we want a story that will explain what reality is all about and what my particular role is in the cosmic drama. This role makes me a part of something bigger than myself, and gives meaning to all my experiences and choices."[17]

As a historian, Harari points out that this human tendency to think in stories isn't always a positive thing. People aren't just heroes or villains. Wars and geopolitics aren't an easily understood single narrative. **Events in real life don't have tidy happy endings.** The world is complex and nuanced— that's precisely the reason humans created stories to help us process it.

---

17 *21 Lessons for the 21st Century*, Yuval Noah Harari (2018)

Our stories can't always capture that complexity, but they should do their best and acknowledge when and where they fall short.

Overly narrow stories can be used to manipulate because they miss out on important context. Be careful how you present narratives that reinforce stereotypes or falsehoods. It can be too easy to do if you're not paying careful enough attention. The narratives we tell one another can be misleading if they're crafted with ill-intent. **Stories are powerful tools. Like all tools, they're neutral.** They're neither good nor bad, but can be used for both. It all depends on who is wielding the narrative. Do your part to ensure that your stories are only used for good.

How to Edit Stories

Find Your Focus

One of the keys to a successful story edit is finding the details that are necessary for moving a story forward. Then get rid of the rest. Start by finding your story's purpose. What are you trying to say? Focus on that target and remove as many distractions from that focus as possible.

Finding that focus may not be something you have from the beginning. You may not discover the true purpose of what you're trying to say until after your second or third draft. You might think you know the story's focus, but it could change as you go along. Some stories never find their purpose. These are the stories that aren't effective or memorable.

This is one way organizational storytelling is unique. Fictional storytellers have the luxury of inventing the details that are relevant to their narrative. **As a business storyteller,**

you have a responsibility to tell true stories, which means finding the real-life details that matter to your audience.

Leaving in anything that isn't relevant to a story's character or conflict can be a distraction. These details might be funny or interesting to you, but they might be something that confuses your audience.

As novelist Stephen King once said, "Kill your darlings." By that he meant, get rid of those things which might be precious to you, but which the audience doesn't care about. Novelist Elmore Leonard meant something similar when he said, "Leave out the boring parts."

Find the Tone

Imagine the Disney family classic *Mary Poppins* as a dark horror film. Visualize Stephen King's famed horror film *IT* as an uplifting family comedy. What would it look like if the biblical epic *Passion of the Christ* was a kung-fu action flick? Or how would the sci-fi comedy *Back to the Future* hold up as an LGBTQ+ romance?

As outlandish as these may sound, these reimagined classic movies are the subjects of re-cut movie trailers scattered across the internet. YouTube and digital video editors have made it possible for nearly anyone to scramble film clips into a new genre—all it requires is an idea and way too much time on your hands.

These re-cut trailers are so prevalent and entertaining because of the stark contrast of tone. Disney's beloved British nanny as a slasher villain is a big jump. *IT's* terrifying demon as a lovable birthday clown requires a serious mental shift. But these leaps are possible by setting a new tone.

Each of these re-cut movie trailers features a new assembly

of cherry-picked scenes, new title cards, and a new music soundtrack. These elements combine to establish a unique characteristic compared to the original film. **Reassembling elements and editing in new details can set or completely shift the tone of your story.** When the creators behind *Toy Story* reworked Woody to be softer and more sympathetic, it changed the entire tone of the film. Adjusting small but crucial details like that can have a significant impact on how your audience experiences the story. **Before you begin crafting a story, know what tone you're trying to set.** What emotions do you want to stir in your audience—humor, fear, sadness, joy? What adjectives do you hope will be used to describe the narrative? Knowing what target you're aiming for should guide how you craft your message—what words, sounds, and visuals are used.

How you craft a story will determine the tone it sets when shared. Use your story's purpose to set the tone and build toward that through editing and assembly.

Find Some Perspective

Regardless of your content (what the story says) or medium (where the story is shared), it takes time to craft an effective narrative.

As the storyteller, you'll know the details of your story better than anyone else (except for perhaps the subject of the story). This is a huge benefit for telling the story. But it can be a liability when it comes to crafting it. As novelist, essayist, and historian Stephen Koch said: "If the story you hear back is something other than the story you told—you will learn where to revise."

To balance this closeness, you've got to find some distance. Take some time after you complete the first draft to clear your mind. Let your story (and yourself) rest before returning to it. Depending on what the story will be used for, that might mean a few hours or a few weeks.

Once you're ready to get back to the story, imagine yourself in the shoes of your audience. Print out the written story and read it aloud. Watch the first draft of the video you created. Listen to the audio story you're trying to tell. Do your best to find objectivity. Make notes of what you notice, but continue to observe the story from an outside perspective.

Get Some Help

Finding an objective perspective is a challenge. You can't (and shouldn't) try to tell your business' story alone. You need some help. That might mean asking someone else on your team or someone outside of your organization.

Involving different people will bring a new perspective to the story you're trying to tell. Not to mention the fact that an objective third party is usually able to spot that obvious misspelling that you overlooked because you were too focused on getting the details right.

In other words, you might need to practice sharing the story during the editing process. That's exactly what George Lucas did with *Star Wars* when he showed a rough draft with his director friends. Their fresh eyes helped him find and fix some glaring story issues.

Writer Jeff Goins claims that writers can't edit their own work—at least not completely. We can catch the occasional typo, but we're too close to this thing that we've created.

"As you compose and craft, like any good parent does with a child, you don't see your work for what it is," says Goins. "You see it for its potential, for what you imagine it to be. In other words, you're blind to reality. To the fact that you left out a word (or several), missed a comma here, and so forth. You need some fresh perspective."[18]

Storytelling is a team sport. Our stories are made better when we invite more people into the process. However, this is also a balance. Too many opinions can overburden the process and generate a story that sounds like it was created by a committee. Finding the right number of people and the right individuals takes time and practice. But it's worth getting right.

If you've been paying attention, you're hopefully already on your way to building a Story Team within your organization. Anyone on this team can provide an outside perspective on what's working (or what's not) in your content. Share your drafts with the team (either individually or as a group) to get constructive feedback and strengthen the narrative.

---

18 Why Writers Can't Edit Their Own Work, Jeff Goins [https://goinswriter.com/writers-cant-edit/]

In Summary

- Stories shouldn't be shared in their raw form. You need to take the time to refine and polish it into something your audience will understand.

- This process takes two large steps: assembling the rough pieces into an order that resembles a narrative and editing those pieces to smooth over the rough edges.

- Assembling a narrative requires understanding what details to include (or leave out) and the scope of the story you're telling.

- Editing the story means you first find a clear message to focus on, set the right tone, determine the perspective to tell the story from, and then seek feedback from others.

- Failing to craft your story leads to a messy final product that will confuse your audience. You owe your story's subject and audience the time to get it right.

CHAPTER 6

SHARE THE STORY

Big Idea: After listening and crafting, a story is ready to be shared.

Have You Met Ted?

The year was 1984 and Harry Marks had an idea. As an award-winning broadcaster, Marks interviewed people in a variety of industries, including design and budding technologies. As these fields of business began to collide, Marks thought about combining these into a new type of event.

But not just another boring conference or tradeshow. Those were fine, but this would be unique. Marks pitched his new event as the "anti-conference."

"I worked with musicians. I worked with artists. I worked with designers. I worked with scientists. I worked with engineers," said Marks. "And it struck me at one point that we were ... bringing these very divergent technologies together. I came up with this idea that I wanted to do a conference, but I didn't know how to."[19]

Marks approached renowned architect Richard Saul Wurman with his idea and asked for help. Wurman loved the idea and agreed to assist, on the condition that they could be equal partners in the enterprise.

Their first event took place in Monterrey, California. Rather than the typical boring conference with slide decks and sponsor booths, Wurman and Marks envisioned the "ultimate dinner party" with cool guests and interesting conversations.

Wurman served as the emcee for the evening. There were no set speeches—just brilliant people taking the stage to talk about things that fascinated and inspired them. The event included a demonstration of the first compact disc, an early Macintosh computer, and a new 3D graphics display from Lucasfilm (yep, the same people who created *Star Wars* and eventually *Pixar*).

Despite the big names and cool vibes, the event ended up as a financial failure. Thankfully, Marks didn't see it as a failure, but rather as a proof of concept. The creators lost money, but they didn't lose hope.

"It totally worked," Marks said. "It didn't work financially for us at all, but it worked in principle."

Six years later, in 1990, they organized another "anti-conference". This time, the idea stuck. The organizers made it work financially and they've held the event every year ever since.

---

19 Remembering Harry Marks, co-founder of the TED Conference, Emily McManus, April 26, 2019 [https://blog.ted.com/remembering-harry-marks-co-founder-of-the-ted-conference]

Share the Story

Since it was a combination of Technology, Education, and Design, the founders created an acronym and called their event the TED Conference. Although it's changed locations and ownership since the early days, TED Talks have continued to have an increasing impact on our culture and education. Every TED speaker has a maximum of 18 minutes to share their carefully crafted thoughts on a specific subject. All of these talks are recorded and uploaded to be shared with the world online. Although not everyone can attend a TED event, anyone with an internet connection can still learn from these stories and ideas.

Each of these events embodies the TED slogan of "ideas worth spreading."

The online TED Talk videos surpassed the one billion view mark (and counting) in 2021. The most popular TED Talk (on why schools kill creativity by multiple-time TED speaker Ken Robinson) has been viewed over 71 million times alone.[20]

In addition to the main annual conference (now held in Vancouver, British Columbia), there are thousands of independent TEDx events organized around the globe. They're built around a specific location or topic. TEDx Conferences expand the number of ideas being shared exponentially.

The story of TED proves the concept of the Story Cycle— **great stories inspire more great stories.** Thousands of TED speakers have shared their stories. Thousands of people in person and millions of more online have absorbed these ideas and allowed them to shape their own stories.

Each time you share a story—whether your own or someone

20   Do schools kill creativity?, Sir Ken Robinson (February 2006) [https://www.ted.com/talks/sir_ken_robinson_do_schools_kill_creativity]

else's—you have the opportunity to inspire, change a life, and generate a new wrinkle in the story of your audience.

Story Sharing

Most people directly equate stories with storytelling. This tracks because there would be no stories without people sharing them. When we think of stories, we envision our history of ancient people sitting around campfires sharing stories.

Story Sharing is the most visible part of the Story Cycle because it's where your organization and audience connect. **Stories come to life when they're shared with others.**

However, keeping the Story Cycle spinning is far more than just storytelling. The telling is where the baton is passed from your organization to the audience. But that's just the tip of the iceberg. There's so much more that goes into capturing and crafting stories to make sharing them possible. That's the essential idea at the core of this book.

Most storytelling books and resources focus almost exclusively on the Story Sharing aspect of the Story Cycle. That's understandable given how crucial and visible the Sharing phase is. These works discuss in-depth how to write your story in a book or a public speech. These are fantastic resources to learn from and valuable skills to develop.

To balance the scales, we're putting Story Sharing in the right perspective with the rest of the Story Cycle Phases. **You can't tell a great story without capturing and curating stories.** And examining the audience's experience with a story (which we'll get to) is an often-overlooked piece of the puzzle. You need to spend at least as much time on those other phases as you do with Story Sharing.

The Story Cycle is a chain—every link is important to keeping the entire process working. Any missed step breaks the cycle and shuts down the story machine. Each step builds on the others.

Nevertheless, Story Sharing is a pivotal moment in the Story Cycle. People directly experience your storytelling. It's the piece they remember. It's supported by each previous step, but the Sharing is where the rubber meets the road.

Business leaders sometimes struggle with this phase for this reason. **Story Sharing is a highly visible and vulnerable practice.** Writing is challenging and public speaking is scary. Holding the collective attention of an entire group of people—whether in person or just on paper—is intimidating. Expressing your personal narrative or being entrusted to do so by others is daunting.

But someone has to step up and be the storyteller. Otherwise, a story will go untold. And that can be even more deadly than your fear of public speaking.

Those Publishers Were Dunces

On March 26, 1969, a relatively unknown man named John Kennedy Toole committed suicide by running a garden hose from the exhaust pipe through the window of his car outside of Biloxi, Mississippi, and the world (especially the storytelling world) was poorer for it.

His car and body were discovered by police officers who noted that his person and the vehicle were remarkably clean, and that "his face showed no signs of distress." Toole was buried in Greenwood Cemetery in his native New Orleans.

Although it's speculative, historians presume that Toole's suicide had to do with his failure to get a book published.

A manuscript for that book was discovered two years later by his mother, Thelma Toole, on top of an armoire in her son's room. From that day forward, it became her mission to get the book published. She viewed it as her way to redeem her son and the act he'd committed.

Over the next five years, Thelma submitted the book to seven different publishers. Each time, she got the same response as her son—a rejection. Each rejection weighed upon Thelma in the same way they had on John Kennedy Toole. But she was determined.

There's a term for this in the media industry: *development hell*. It's usually when a film or other creative project is continually kicked around in various stages of production, with seemingly no hope of seeing the light of the public eye.

Except, in most cases, this situation is endured by a team of creatives who have been deferred because of some bureaucratic or other reason. Toole endured his own version of developmental hell completely alone. He knew how good his book was, but no one else acknowledged it. There's no wonder he experienced despair and disappointment.

After persistence bordering on harassment, Thelma Toole finally got her son's book published by the Louisiana State University Press in 1980—eleven years after its author took his own life, and sixteen years after he had finished writing the manuscript.

Although the initial print run was only 2,500 copies, it didn't take long for *The Confederacy of Dunces* to gain attention in the literary world. By the next year, Toole was posthumously awarded the Pulitzer Prize for Fiction. The book has since been adapted into a stage play—and so has the story of Toole's life and his efforts to get his work published. In 2019, the BBC included *The Confederacy of Dunces* on its list of the 100 most influential novels in history.

This backstory of one of my favorite novels is the story of perseverance, a dream deferred, and long-awaited vindication. In our context, it's also an example of the importance of sharing your story—and how difficult that occasionally can be.

We take for granted how easy it is to reach an audience today. Had John Kennedy Toole had access to the internet, would he have needed to wait so long to find his audience? Would he have suffered needlessly to unveil his creative talent to the world?[21]

A Confederacy of Dunces is not the only classic piece of literature that nearly wasn't published.

- Stephen King tossed what would be his first novel, *Carrie,* into the wastebasket before his wife made him retrieve it and keep working.

- Harper Lee threw her manuscript of *To Kill a Mockingbird* out into the snow but her friend Truman Capote encouraged her to persevere.

- Theodore Gisell would never have become Dr. Seuss had he followed through on his promise to burn the pages of his first book, *And To Think That I Saw It on Mulberry Street.*

---

21 These questions are rhetorical for a reason. It's tough to grapple with 'what if' scenarios like this—especially when suicide is involved. They're not meant to diminish or oversimplify the decision Toole made. If you're experiencing similar hopelessness, please get help.

Not being able to share the story inside of you can be frustrating and disheartening. This is true for creative artists who write best-selling novels. It's also true for business leaders who hope to tell the world about the difference they can make. We all yearn to share our narrative and feel heard by someone.

Your story isn't complete until you tell it.

Unshared Stories

"Real artists ship," is a quote often attributed to visionary Apple co-founder Steve Jobs—which likely means he didn't actually say it.[22] Nevertheless, there is some truth in the axiom.

Essentially, you can't call yourself an artist unless you produce art. You can't call yourself a writer unless you write. **You can't call yourself a storyteller unless you tell stories.**

It's not enough to just Story Listen and fill your Story Library with unheard tales. It's not enough to Story Craft, but never feel confident enough to share until the narrative is perfect—because it never will be. **Your audience deserves to have their stories shared.** They want to hear great stories of people just like them. Not for your business's sake, but for their own.

At the risk of sounding obvious, **a story that's not shared won't have an impact.** All of the work to capture and craft a story becomes meaningless without finding the right method of passing it along to a captive audience.

---

22 Probably Wozniak said it first, but Jobs just said it better.

It's easy to get caught in perfectionism when trying to craft the story in just the right way. Or wait until you have just the right detail to include. Or wait until just the right moment to share the story. Just as easily, you can get caught in the anxiety of not wanting to mess up the story with subpar storytelling skills. What if you're not able to do it justice?

These are relatable and understandable excuses, but they're still just excuses. You must trust yourself to get the story right. Knowing when a story is ready to be shared is an instinct that comes with practice. The truth is that you might mess it up or the story might be less than perfect. But that's still better than the story that no one ever gets to hear.

As Maya Angelou said, "There is no greater agony than bearing an untold story inside you." Perhaps that's what pushed John Kennedy Toole to take his own life—because he had endured the agony of not being able to share his novel with others.

The stories you have the privilege of sharing are not your own. They are the tales of the men and women you serve with your business. Getting to share their stories is a responsibility not to be taken lightly. In doing so, you release the tension of their stories going unshared. You grant them the honor of bringing light to their life and amplifying their voice.

That's why these stories are worth sharing, and the risks that come with shirking this responsibility.

A Hurricane of a Story

Rubin Carter was trying to make something of his life.

He'd had a troubling childhood that included a stint in juvenile detention. Carter joined the U.S. Army but was discharged as being unfit for military service. After returning home to New Jersey, he was convicted of mugging and spent time in prison.

Upon being released, Carter channeled his bad behavior in the boxing ring. He quickly became one of the most formidable middleweight boxers in the country. His aggression and powerful style earned him the nickname "Hurricane." Boxing finally gave Rubin Carter the outlet he needed to turn his life around.

In the wee hours of the morning of June 17, 1966, Carter and his friend were driving home in Paterson, New Jersey. Police pulled their car over and hauled the two African-American men down to the station. The authorities questioned Carter and his friend for 17 hours about the details of a triple murder committed at a nearby bar earlier that morning.

Because they matched eye-witness descriptions of the murderers, Carter and his friend was tried and convicted of the crime. "Hurricane" Carter went from being the favorite to win a boxing title to serving a life sentence in Rahway State Prison.

Thankfully, that's not where Rubin Carter's story ends.

Nineteen years later, a retrial found the boxer innocent of all charges. Rubin Carter was finally released from prison in 1988—22 years after he was wrongfully put in prison for a crime he didn't commit. Over a decade of those years were spent in solitary confinement. It was an injustice egregious enough to inspire a story, or perhaps several.

Rubin Carter published his autobiography, *The Sixteenth Round*, in 1974, while still in prison. The book outlines his difficult upbringing and stood as a cry for help of his innocence. Others were willing to share his story, too.

After reading the memoir and visiting Carter in prison, folk singer Bob Dylan released an eight-minute-long single entitled *Hurricane*, an overt protest about Carter's wrongful conviction.

Years later, a young Denzel Washington portrayed Carter in the 1999 film, *The Hurricane*—a role for which Washington earned a best actor Golden Globe. Author Ken Klonsky shared an updated version of Carter's story in his 2011 book, *The Eye of the Hurricane*. And the BBC released a 13-part podcast series in 2019 called *The Hurricane Tapes*, which included hours of interviews with eyewitnesses and even Rubin Carter himself.

So, what lesson can The Hurricane's story teach us beyond some of the racial injustices in our justice system? **A good story can be shared far and wide.** It doesn't have to be told once and then forgotten about. The right story can be told in books, podcasts, movies, and songs. When you've done the work to craft a meaningful story, make sure that it's told repeatedly.

Where to Share a Story

As we've established, context is crucial for a good story. **The medium you use to share the story shapes the message itself.**[23] There are two main categories for how to share a story: spoken and written.

Spoken includes everything from in-person speeches to oral storytelling. But this also extends to video and audio forms. These primarily involve visual elements—except for

23 Thanks, Marshall Mcluhan

audio-only formats, like podcasting. Written stories are those that primarily rely on textbooks, blog posts, and the like.

Because these forms will be consumed differently, they allow you to craft the story differently. You'll reach new sections of your audience with each medium. And the capabilities and limitations will be different for each.

Keep in mind, that spoken stories like TED Talks still have a written component. If you're presenting on stage or through a video, you'll need to write a script first. Conversely, written pieces can incorporate visual elements, too. Books like *A Confederacy of Dunces* can include images and blog posts can embed videos.

Best of all, you're able to share effective stories in multiple mediums, just like Rubin "Hurricane" Carter's tale of wrongful imprisonment found life in song, book, and podcast series.

You have the opportunity to mix and match elements of both written and spoken stories. **A good narrative is like gas; it adapts to fit the shape that you put it into.**

When to Share a Story

When the American sports network ESPN turned 30 years old, two well-known sports journalists, Bill Simmons and Connor Schell, decided to give the world the gift of more sports stories.

Two years before the network's milestone birthday, Simmons and Schell (both ESPN contributors) concocted the idea of a documentary series to commemorate three decades of inspiring sports stories. They envisioned 30 short films, created by 30 directors, to tell 30 of the best stories in athletics since 1979.

On October 6, 2009, *Kings Ransom* aired on ESPN and its

sister networks—telling the story of how Wayne Gretsky's 1988 blockbuster trade to the Los Angeles Kings shaped the landscape of the National Hockey League and the Great One's career.

Twenty-nine other documentary films followed over the next twelve months—ranging from stories about Nelson Mandela and the 1995 South African rugby team championship to Colombian soccer star Andrés Escobar's connection with Columbian drug lord Pablo Escobar. These real-life stories demonstrated the real-life impact that sports can have on culture and the world around them.

But those first 30 films weren't enough.

It's nearly impossible to cover the full scope of sports in a mere 30 segments. So the *30 For 30* series was renewed for another season. Then it was renewed again. It has since been spun off into a series called *ESPN Films Presents*, as well as a series of shorter documentaries.

All told, this simple idea has spawned more than 150 different stories (and counting). Despite low popularity with the first few installations, viewership and critical acclaim have steadily grown. *30 For 30* films have won two Peabody Awards, an Emmy, and even the Academy Award for Best Documentary Feature with their 2016 expose on O.J. Simpson.

What turned into a birthday present to the nation's most popular sports network has grown into something much broader. It's become ESPN's most powerful engine for telling the industry's greatest narratives.

The success of *30 For 30* teaches us something about storytelling—timing matters. **When and how often you share stories makes a difference in how these stories are received.**

You can't only communicate in stories—that sounds like the backstory for a mysterious old sea hermit in a Scooby-Doo episode. Stories are like fruit—they're healthy and delicious, but that's not all you can eat. You must have some variety in your diet.

Therefore, when and how often you share stories is a key component of your organizational story strategy. This means focusing on two things: timing and frequency.

Timing comes down too many different factors, so there is no single recipe for when. When doesn't mean the time of year or day, but where, in the cadence of your communication, a story falls. However, it's a good rule of thumb to start your communication with a narrative. With a speech, video, or book, you're trying to grab your audience's attention immediately. And a story is one of the most effective ways to do so.

Even better, try opening a Story Loop at the beginning. Create suspense. Make the audience wonder what will happen in your story so they continue to pay attention to you. Don't deliver the payoff of the story until after you've delivered your key point. Conclude your presentation with the resolution to the story. That's not always easy or feasible, but it's effective in keeping people focused.

As for frequency, **don't be afraid to share a good story multiple times, on various mediums**. People need to hear a message multiple times before they'll remember it. They'll likely need to hear it less often if it's shared with a story. Spread one example of an organizational story across several of your marketing channels—video, social media, website, etc.

Even if the same person hears the same story in different places, it reinforces the same message. Besides, stories can be shared in new ways on different channels. So, the video client testimonial will be experienced differently than when your audience sees it as an infographic on social media or reads it on your company blog.

There's a fine balance between under-sharing and oversharing a specific story, but most organizations under-share. Perhaps that's because they're not confident enough in the quality of the work. Or they've grown bored with the story themselves. Remember that once you've heard the story internally a few dozen times, it likely means that your audience has only heard it once or twice. Keep sharing.

Who Shares the Story

To this point, your Story Team has collected and crafted the story. Now it's time to share it. This task is placed on the shoulders of the storyteller. That person's role will vary based on where you're sharing the story.

If it's a written piece, the storyteller is likely the person writing the first draft. If it's a spoken piece, then it's the storyteller who speaks on stage or in front of the camera. These could be different people.

Regardless of where the story is being shared, who should the storyteller be? More specifically, what skills and traits does the ideal storyteller possess? There are three specific attributes—**clarity, confidence, and caring**—to look for (or hone) as you're preparing to deliver the story to your audience.

Clarity

In 1944, the United States Air Force began to bomb Japan in the hopes of ending World War II. The American bomber planes flew high over the Japanese islands but kept missing their targets badly. Something was wrong. An onboard military meteorologist discovered that 200+ mile-per-hour winds were pushing the planes faster than in recorded history. At the time, that seemed impossible.

These days, we have a name for those high-altitude, high-speed winds—the Jet Stream. It was a revolutionary find. But the U.S. Air Force wasn't the first to discover the Jet Stream—just the first to clearly communicate their findings.

The global air current was originally discovered 18 years earlier by Japanese meteorologist Wasaburo Oishi. Oishi completed over 1,300 experiments observing the high-altitude wind stream before publishing a paper on it in 1926. Normally, a paper like that would have caused an international stir. It would have made Oishi famous, at least in the scientific community. But in his case, no one noticed. Why not?

Because besides being a meteorologist, Oishi was a dedicated Esperantist—someone who speaks Esperanto, an artificial language created in the 1870s. And Oishi published his groundbreaking paper on the Jet Stream in Esperanto.

Esperanto has a small but dedicated following. An estimated 100,000 people globally speak some degree of the language, but the numbers were much smaller in 1926. Enough so that a groundbreaking scientific discovery published in the obscure language could go largely ignored for decades.

Oishi's example teaches us that **we must speak the same language as our audience.** That doesn't just mean the general language like English or Spanish—it also means the nuances of language like word choice and dialect.

Good storytellers understand how their audience speaks and adjust their voices to match.

Confidence

He lives vicariously through himself.

He's been known to cure narcolepsy, just by walking into a room.

He's a lover, not a fighter, but he's also a fighter, so don't get any ideas.

The police often question him, just because they find him interesting.

He once had an awkward moment, just to see how it feels.

He is the Most Interesting Man in the World.

He was also the iconic face of Dos Equis beer for over a decade in a critically-acclaimed and wildly popular advertising campaign for the Mexican beer company. With a list of attributes rivaled only by Chuck Norris for internet meme supremacy, "The Most Interesting Man in the World" certainly had ample confidence and charisma.

Storytellers can learn a few things from Dos Equis about confidence. "The Most Interesting Man in the World" campaign was a bold character to introduce, but it paid off. It showed faith in their brand, but also in their ability to pull off a fun campaign that would represent them well.

Part of that shows in TMIMITW's (boy, that's a long acronym) catchphrase: *"I don't always drink beer, but when I do, I prefer Dos Equis."* They had the clarity to know that a guy this interesting is going to prefer tequila. He's not going to tie himself to one beer brand. They had enough humility to keep it realistic—at least as realistic as a guy who lives vicariously through himself.

By the way, Dos Equis' indomitable ad campaign is among the few examples of a business successfully leveraging a fictional story. Believe it or not, "The Most Interesting Man in the World" doesn't actually exist (gasp!), but was created by a marketing agency for the Mexican beer company. The goal was to build a fake character that represents the whimsical and bold nature of Dos Equis. When it comes to this level of creativity, it's often wise to trust this to the professionals.

Anyone who shares the stories for your brand should do their best to embody this same confidence as "The Most Interesting Man in the World." Both the confidence that the story is worth telling and confidence in their own ability to share it. Otherwise, you're stuck stammering and shuffling in front of your audience, which is an unneeded distraction.

Practice your storytelling. Sharpen your skills. Develop your craft. And if all else fails, drink a few beers before going on stage.

Caring

The exhibit looked like a giant shoebox. Which was appropriate, because it was filled with other people's shoes. The giant shoe box was also filled with their stories—primarily photographs and audio recordings of more than 30 people who worked in and use the British health care system.

Titled *A Mile in My Shoes*, the immersive exhibit was a partnership between the United Kingdom's Health Foundation and The Empathy Museum. On display back in 2016, the award-winning exhibit gave visitors an insight into what it was like to be a doctor, pharmacist, or parametric.

Visitors were invited to slip on a pair of shoes, donated by the real people featured in the audio recordings. The goal was to build empathy for these healthcare workers and help to expand the public's perspective on the practice of medicine.

"I walked in Becky's shoes, a working mom caring for a little boy with severe learning difficulties," said Jayne Chidgey-Clark, a clinical associate in the England National Health Service. "Looking down and thinking that she'd worn these shoes in her struggles made me really be able to hear her story and really empathize with her."[24]

Empathy and caring are crucial parts of the entire Story Cycle, but no more than during the sharing process. This is when your organization interacts most directly with your audience. They're looking to you for guidance. Only by responding to them with understanding and sensitivity will you earn their trust. This goes for both the audience and the people whose stories you're sharing.

Include details in your story to show that you know who you're speaking to. Speak to them with respect and dignity, no matter who they are. It's not enough to say you care about them, you must show that you do. There's a balance to strike between caring and confidence, but it's one worth finding.

Passing the Torch

Every modern Olympic Games starts with a traditional torch run that carries the eternal flame from Athens, Greece to the current Olympic host. During the Summer games, there are

---

24   A Mile in My Shoes at the Houses of Parliament, (October 2016) [https://www.youtube.com/watch?v=d8TgG6KvqI0]

several relay events on the track. In both instances, there's something important being passed hand-to-hand, runner-to-runner, person-to-person.

Whether it's a baton or a torch or a narrative, the hand-off is crucial.

Every story shared is a hand-off—sharing the burning idea in your mind with another's mind. **Storytelling is the movement of ideas from internal to external.** If you're successful in the transfer, the fire of inspiration sparks in the other's brain and shines all the brighter.

Storytelling is especially effective because you're not only passing the torch from one to one; you have the opportunity (especially in organizational storytelling) to ignite conceptual fires in the minds of thousands, a veritable bonfire. That's how movements are started and the world is changed—through the collective spreading of great ideas and the inspiration to act on them.

"All of us have been given stories by other people. Stories passed on to us by our families and others in generations before us. Almost everything we know has been given to us in the form of a story."[25]

The task before you is to pass the proverbial torch into the hands of your audience.

- Through **Story Listening**, you seek out the glowing embers of those whose story has not yet been heard.

- Through **Story Crafting**, you stoke those fires to allow them to burn brighter and control the flames to be used for **a purpose.**

25   Yanu Endar Prasetyo. *From Storytelling to Social Change: The Power of Story in the Community Building.* (2017)

- Through **Story Sharing**, you invite others to gather around the fire and experience the warmth of the story for themselves.

What happens next is dependent upon how you've set up the story. Now it's time for everyone to light their torches and carry them back home. But there's an inevitable element of random chance at play, too. Will the story resonate with your audience? Will they remember it? Will it have the intended effect?

This is the point where most storytelling books end. You've shared the story and now there's seemingly nothing else you can do. Except, there is. There's no perfect way to understand what happens when you pass along the torch, but there are strategies to give us an idea. There's no way to read your audience's mind, but there are ways to watch how they respond. There's no true method for measuring our story's impact, but there are methods to watch how people's lives are changed and practice telling those stories, too.

This is when we flip the Story Cycle over to the other half of the equation. We've focused on our organization as the guide, but it's time to think about the hero of the story—your audience.

- Once you've collected and crafted your story, you have a compulsion (and obligation) to share it with the right audience.

- The process of developing stories is much more than sharing. However, this is easily the most compelling part because it's where stories come to life.

- Unshared stories are left to die because this stops the Story Cycle. Being unable to share a story can harm us, too.

- Thankfully, stories can be shared through nearly any medium (and sometimes all of them). But where you share the story impacts how you tell it, and how it's received.

- When to share the story and who takes on the role of storyteller are also significant considerations for your organization.

PART 3

CONNECTING THE STORY TO THE REAL HERO

"Storytelling helps the audience understand its world,
and motivates them to improve it"
— Nell Painter,
Princeton University History Professor

CHAPTER 7

CREATE AN EXPERIENCE

Big Idea: Your story must draw your audience into a memorable experience for it to make a lasting impact.

Out of the Darkness

Andreas Heinecke was born in southern Germany in 1955. At the age of 13, he learned that part of his mother's family was Jewish, many of whom were killed during the Holocaust.

At the same time, Andreas discovered that parts of his father's family were strong Nazi supporters during the second World War. This dichotomy caused young Heinecke to wonder how people on either side of his family could be so different.

This realization led Heinecke down the path toward social entrepreneurship. He hoped to use a successful business to help culture and make a meaningful impact.

After earning his Ph.D. in philosophy, Heinecke worked at a local radio station in Frankfurt. There, he was tasked with training another young journalist who had recently become blind in a car accident. Heinecke's immediate reaction was pity. He had never met a blind person before and underestimated the young man's capabilities.

"I was literally blown away by his optimism, and the way he coped with the situation," said Heinecke in his 2013 TEDx talk.[26] "He really changed my understanding. Then I was embarrassed because I had judged so surely that this was not a valuable life . . . This was the turning point in my life and I said, 'OK I have to do something'."

Heinecke changed his life because of a chance encounter. He adopted a mantra from the German-Jewish philosopher Martin Buber who said, "The only way to learn is by encounter." In other words, **the only way to truly understand someone else's story is through an experience**.

So Heinecke set out to create similar encounters for others so they might equally be transformed and reach new levels of understanding. His wish was to build a platform to encourage unique experiences and open the chance for meaningful dialogues.

Out of that desire came the realization that darkness reverses the roles of the blind and the sighted. Darkness puts blind people in their element. They're accustomed to operating without sight. Simultaneously, darkness places those of us who can see at a disadvantage. Losing our sight forces us to rely on other senses. We find a new understanding and appreciation for the daily lives of those who cannot see.

Darkness turns the tables and opens the opportunity

---

26 Find Your Place in the Universe, Andreas Heinecke, TEDxAshokaU (2013) [https://www.youtube.com/watch?v=frSwY0xwKO0]

for a transformative experience. Thus, Dialog im Dunkeln (translated to Dialogue in the Dark) was born. The first exhibit opened in Frankfurt, Germany in 1988. The idea was as original as it was simple.

People pay to walk around in dark rooms. The rooms are staged to resemble ordinary scenes—a grocery store, a busy city street, and a neighborhood park. Every group of visitors is led by a blind guide. They're given canes to feel their surroundings. Each participant uses their four other senses to experience what life might be like without vision.

"It's quite a challenge to imagine an enterprise or a business that sells darkness," said Heinecke. "Darkness is universal. Nobody wants to pay for it . . . Secondly, who wants to employ blind people? But when you combine [these] two impossibilities, that's exactly what happened."

These are precisely the things Heinecke set out to achieve— to spread understanding of others' experiences, to employ those who might not otherwise have an opportunity, and to build a sustainable social business that makes an impact.

In the decades since the first Dialogue in the Dark opened, exhibits have visited an additional 150 cities in 30 countries around the world. Over nine million people have experienced the darkness, led by one of the thousands of blind guides that the business employs.

"Dialogue in the Dark is not supposed to simulate blindness," said Heinecke. "It's an opportunity to unite two worlds that don't often have the chance for an exchange."

I walked through a Dialogue in the Dark exhibit several years ago when it came to Atlanta. I vividly remember what it was like to temporarily lose my vision. I remember how it felt to fumble through a dark room, relying only on touch and sound. Those memories are indelible—for me and anyone else who has experienced it.

But bringing light into the darkness was only the beginning.

The Dialogue Social Enterprise, founded by Heinecke and his wife, Orna Cohen, has since created two more similar exhibitions: Dialogue in Silence and Dialogue in Time.

Dialogue in Silence is an experience in soundproof rooms, forcing people to communicate through non-verbal methods like hand gestures, facial expressions, and body language. Dialogue in Time features guides over 70 years of age helping younger audience members to think differently about older generations.

Together, these three experiences give everyone the chance to walk a mile in someone else's story. Opportunities like these are transformational.

Experiencing a Story

Great stories invite you into the narrative. They engage your senses and stir your emotions. Great stories are memorable because they feel as if you were physically present with the characters.

We used to live in the Information Age when knowledge was power. But that age is effectively over. Information is easily and cheaply accessible. The new form of social currency is our attention. Infinite knowledge is a mere Google search away. But holding someone's attention is a challenge.[27]

---

27 Hey, look down here at this! See how distracting that was?

Stories are no longer about communicating pieces of information. They're a powerful vehicle for sharing an experience, connecting people through emotion, and building empathy across growing cultural barriers. **Stories are one of the best ways to attract attention** and are therefore a vital skill for any business leader.

Bantam Books started publishing the *Choose Your Own Adventure* series of gamebooks back in 1976. Over the next twelve years, they published over 180 different interactive books for a young-adult audience. The concept came from Edward Packard, who was inspired by the bedtime stories he used to tell his daughters. When he ran out of ideas for what the protagonist should do, he would ask his daughters and then adapt the story accordingly.

In 2018, these books crossed into another popular interactive storytelling platform: video games. That's when Z-Man Games licensed the *Choose Your Own Adventure* name for their series of games inspired by the series.

The concept has even spilled over into traditionally less interactive mediums. In 2019, Netflix released its first interactive film: *Black Mirror: Bandersnatch*. At points in the film, the viewer is given a choice as to how the movie should proceed. Just like the *Choose Your Own Adventure* books, these decisions impact the outcome of the story.

You can even think about the growing fad of escape rooms as another example of interactive and experiential storytelling. It's clear from these examples that **people want to play an active role in the stories that they hear**. It's also clear that budding technology is making this easier than ever.

Virtually There

You are a young, pregnant woman. You are sitting in a doctor's office. The doctor approaches and asks you questions about how you're feeling. She can tell you're uncomfortable because of what you recently experienced. A few minutes earlier, while driving to the healthcare clinic, you are accosted by protestors with picket signs. They hurl hurtful taunts and jeers at you. They call you cruel names and say you'll burn in hell.

You are a teenage African American boy. You're in an average bedroom, your room. You look at yourself in the mirror. You reflect on moments in your life from adolescence to adulthood—everything from talking with your mother in the living room to going on a job interview. You play with other kids your age. You also have an encounter with the police. Each of these moments feels familiar, but also different. Perhaps because everyone else you interact with is white and looks different from you.

You are a prisoner in solitary confinement. You are alone in a cell that measures six feet by nine feet—a total of 54 square feet. The walls are bare, beige concrete blocks. There is a small wall-mounted cot in one corner, a grimy metal toilet in the opposite corner, and a slab of a desk along one wall. On the desk are a few books. There is a solid metal door and a slim window that lets through a hint of daylight. You've spent the past 23 hours in that room without seeing or hearing from another human being.

You are homeless. You were laid off two months ago and couldn't afford your housing expenses. You sold most of your possessions to try and pay rent but were still unable to cover the costs. You end up living in your car, where all of your remaining possessions clutter the seats. Multiple tickets from the police force you to sell your car to avoid jail time. You're forced to spend most of your time on public transportation and off the streets. You are not the only homeless person who rides the bus each night as their only shelter.

These are true stories you can experience nearly firsthand. That's because each of these narratives was developed into virtual reality (or VR) interactive documentaries by several nonprofits. The goal of each one is to place viewers into the shoes of those in need. The hope is that placing others into the perspective of these vulnerable populations will spark empathy and begin a shift in our culture.

Many of these VR experiences were studied by journalist Kaitlin Ugolik Phillips in her 2020 book, *The Future of Feeling*. "Few people reported having immediate life-changing epiphanies," said Phillips. "But many say they feel disturbed and inspired enough to start thinking about something a bit differently."[28]

The Tow Center of Digital Journalism reported that "stories experienced in VR prompted a higher empathetic response than static photo/text treatments and a higher likelihood of participants to take a 'political or social action' after viewing." In other words, virtual reality doesn't change someone or their mind about a topic, but it does open them to new ways of thinking on an issue.

The first story of a young woman going to an abortion clinic is called "Across the Line" and was developed by Planned Parenthood. Although the people you see in the virtual reality video are animated, their voices are actual

---

28   *The Future of Feeling: Building Empathy in a Tech-Obsessed World*, Kaitlin Ugolik Phillips pg. 67 (2020)

recordings experienced by real women. Regardless of your views on abortion, the immersive narrative is eye-opening.

The second story of the young African-American man was entitled "1,000 Cut Journey". The title represents the countless minor ways minorities experience racism in everyday life. The project premiered at the Tribeca Film Festival in 2018 and was created by the Virtual Human Interaction Lab at Stanford University.

The third story of the prisoner in solitary confinement is the 2016 product of *The Guardian* newspaper in Britain. Its title is a reference to the size of those cells: "6x9". Not only do audience members see themselves in the small cell, but they also hear recordings of the voices of real people who endured solitary confinement. It's easy to view prisoners as criminals, but they're people, too.

The final story was also produced by the Stanford Virtual Human Interaction Lab. Titled "Being Homeless: A Human Experience", this seven-minute immersive 360-degree video walks people through the different stages of what sends normal people into life without a home. Most of us know what homeless people look like, but we rarely know how they ended up in their circumstances.

None of these high-tech projects are the same as being there—it's not the same as getting an abortion, being racially profiled, getting thrown in solitary confinement, or being homeless. But these narratives are one step closer to helping a wider group reach a new level of understanding. Each narrative is made more impactful because of the way the organizations leverage new technology to amplify the experience.

Go Big or Go Home

These virtual reality examples are experiential for a few reasons.

- They're **immersive**. There's detail and realism.

- They're **relevant**. They cover issues that are meaningful and interesting to people.

- They're also **relatable**. The audience can see themselves in the protagonists' shoes; that's literally the case with virtual reality stories.

There's another trick that can spark nearly instant experience. **Ask your audience to generate content for you.** Enable them to capture and share their stories themselves. This skips the Story Crafting stage, so you might need to do the editing yourself. But when done well, this generates another level of more genuine stories at a grander scale.

This isn't possible for every business. But there's a well-known example of a business with user-generated stories built into its core. And it all starts with surfing.

Nick Woodman wanted to be an entrepreneur. But he'd crashed and burned with his first two business tries. Frustrated, Woodman moved to Australia to clear his mind and go surfing. He and his surfing buddies dreamed of potentially going pro in surfing but knew they'd need quality photos of themselves shredding the waves to make that happen. However, they ran into snags trying to capture the right images.

Hiring a professional with the right equipment was too expensive. Amateur photographers didn't have the equipment to get quality photos. Woodman couldn't take the photos himself for fear of losing the equipment in the waves. What he needed was a small, lightweight, waterproof camera that a surfer could carry and snap high-quality pics while hanging ten.

With this problem in mind, Woodman moved back to California and got to work on his idea. He sold shell necklaces out of his van to raise money for the venture. Two years later, he had enough seed money and a working product to hit the market.

Woodman worked with local surf shops to spread the word. Gradually, his tiny camera began to gain traction. A couple of years later, the company added video capturing to the still camera. With the increasing popularity of YouTube, these cameras couldn't have come at a better time.

Today, GoPro has more than 90% of the action camera market. They've sold more than 26 million devices and the GoPro name is synonymous with recording adventure stories. There's no doubt that much of this success comes from the incredible videos captured by their adventurous users. **Countless online videos of stunning feats inspire even more adventures**.

Best of all, GoPro doesn't have to capture these videos themselves. They're provided by their community. People don't share these awesome videos to promote the company; they share the videos because the company provided them with a product that helped them look amazing.

There's a direct line between the stories being told and the experiences they capture. GoPro was just smart enough to create a simple device that could connect the two.

An Unexperienced Story

Good stories transport an audience somewhere else. They captivate their minds and senses. However, this is a tenuous grasp—it's far too easy to break the spell and people's attention. This could be from an external source, like a ringing cell phone or a crying baby, or your story itself.

If you confuse your audience or offend them with an inappropriate joke, it'll be that much harder to land your message. There are three primary barriers we're up against when it comes to trying to get an audience to experience a story: **distraction, doubt,** and **disconnection.**

Distraction

In the Disney-Pixar film *Up*, the two protagonists travel to South America where they meet a special golden retriever named Dug. Dug is special not because he's unlike other dogs, but because he wears a special collar that translates his thoughts into speech. And his thoughts are very much what we might imagine hearing from a typical golden retriever.

Dug's catchphrase, which has morphed into an online meme, is interrupting his train of speech with random shouts of 'Squirrel!' The dog has perpetual shiny-object syndrome—or maybe in his case it's bushy-tail syndrome. Dug's simple-minded and easily-distracted nature is funny because it also represents the shortened attention span of people.

Unlike Dug, we're not usually distracted by squirrels (although it is easy to hate those tree-rats). Instead, our shiny objects are cell phones, aimless thoughts, side conversations, and any other urgent, but unimportant things that flash in our minds. You're competing against these distractions any time you share your story.

This shows the brilliance of Dialogue in the Dark. There are practically no distractions in the darkness—neither screens nor squirrels. Every participant in the process is wholly immersed. The exhibit's context lends itself to holding their full attention.

Give your audience a reason to listen to you. If they believe you're boring, it's too late to win back their focus. They've already moved on to the laundry list of other things on their mind. Remember what you're up against and be more interesting and exciting than all the distractions.

Doubt

In speculative fiction, there's a concept known as the "suspension of disbelief" that's crucial for a story to work. Viewers of *Game of Thrones* can't enjoy the layered character development if they're too caught up with the fact dragons don't exist. Readers of *Ender's Game* will miss the compelling character relationships if they're constantly doubting the existence of aliens.

The term was coined by British poet and philosopher Samuel Taylor Coleridge back in 1817. But he was merely recognizing an agreement that has existed between storytellers and audience for as long as fairy tales have been told.

People can realize that your story is false and still enjoy it. Except when you're trying to share a story about your organization. You don't have the benefit of the suspension of disbelief.

People expect your narratives to be true—or at least based in truth and reality. **You must establish a level of trust and confidence in your audience or risk losing them completely.**

Your purpose is not to exclusively entertain with your stories. So, no dragons or aliens for you.

The virtual reality stories we learned about were anonymous but based on reality. It was that reality that made them worth experiencing. The guides of Dialogue in the Dark are blind themselves, which gives them credibility. These organizations minimize the reasons why someone should doubt.

As a keeper of stories for your brand, you have an obligation to the truth. That might mean leaving some details out, changing names for anonymity, or shifting narrative elements around to help things make sense. That's why the Story Crafting process exists. However, that should never infringe on the integrity of your story. Honesty should still be a core value for you.

People are accustomed to being manipulated by advertising and cultural narratives. **We live in a time when doubt is the default and trust must be earned.** If people doubt your motives or the accuracy of your story, you've introduced an impassable barrier. If people think you're trying to slip something past them, there's no way that they'll experience the story the way you want them to.

Disconnection

In the late 1980s, Oldsmobile was failing to connect with younger demographics—and with a name like Oldsmobile, it's not hard to tell why. So, the car manufacturer set out to create an ad campaign that would appeal to a new generation. At least, that was the goal.

The commercials featured celebrities and their kids with the tagline: "This is not your father's Oldsmobile." It sounded like a recipe for success, but the campaign completely backfired. The ads angered their existing customer base by painting them as outdated and unhip. Meanwhile, it failed to connect with younger drivers, who continued to ignore the brand.

The campaign damaged the Oldsmobile brand. Their sales continued to drop and so did customer loyalty. The ad campaign started a steady decline that would see the brand retired by General Motors a decade later. That's some serious disconnection.

Safe to say, **not understanding how your audience views your story can lead to disconnection and negative backlash**. Failing to connect your story with your audience is a step toward going out of business. Like a virtual reality set without a power source, a story without a connection to its intended audience is dead and useless.

Not all stories are relevant to every audience. Not everyone will appreciate or even understand the message you're trying to share. Disconnection between your narrative and the people you're sharing it with brings the Story Cycle to a grinding halt. There's no way to guarantee that your story will resonate completely, but you can still do the work to avoid disaster.

For your audience to experience a story, you must avoid these distractions, doubts, and disconnections. But creating an experience goes beyond that.

How to Make Your Story an Experience

Remember Your Context

Stand-up comedy is one of the most entertaining things you can experience live. The best comedians adjust to mistakes, or even drunk hecklers, and turn it into part of their act. There's a reason why improvisational comedy is especially enjoyable. Not only are you seeing talented artists respond in the moment, but you're also seeing something created that will never happen again.

That's not to say that your story sharing will be as memorable or funny as an improv comedy troupe, but you can still learn from their techniques. Take advantage of your surroundings. Call out specific things to your audience. Mention things about people in the audience or your environment.

These small adjustments not only show that you're comfortable going (slightly) off-script, but that you were willing to give them a custom experience. You've told a story that's special just for them. It's unique, not a copy and paste of your last presentation.

If you're not sharing a story live, remember the context of the platform you're sharing on. An audio story will be a different experience compared to a video one. Find small but impactful ways to create a special moment for that specific platform.

Evoke a Specific Emotion

If anyone knows how to create an experience, it's Steven Spielberg. His multiple accolades and iconic status as a film director speak for themselves. Here's what Spielberg says about experiencing a story:

> "The most amazing thing for me is that every single person who sees a movie, not necessarily one of my movies, brings a whole set of unique experiences, but through careful manipulation and good storytelling, you can get everybody to clap at the same time, to hopefully laugh at the same time, and to be afraid at the same time."[29]

Notice what Spielberg focuses on in his quote: "clap at the same time, laugh at the same time, be afraid at the same time". **A good story can make a group of unique individuals feel the same emotion simultaneously.** Even feelings like happiness, humor, and fear, are powerful emotions.

You can do the same through your organizational storytelling. It's not easy, but it's more attainable with a story. Here's the trick—**you must know what emotion you're going after and focus on it**.

Some stories easily elicit emotions on their own, but you've got to know what emotion that is. Not because you need to overdo it—in fact, you can spoil the moment by being too on the nose. One sure way to wreck being funny or heartfelt is by trying too hard. Conversely, if you're unaware of the sentiment you're stirring in your audience, you run the risk of coming off as tone-deaf.

Don't forget another trigger word that Spielberg used in his quote: "manipulation". Because that's what you're doing

---

29   Entertainment Weekly, December 2011 [https://ew.com/article/2011/12/02/steven-spielberg-ew-interview/]

by using a story to make a group of people feel a certain way. **Stories leverage people's emotions for an outcome.** You can use this power for good, or not. If you attempt to sway people for your own gain and fail, expect them to not be amused.

Experience Stories for Yourself

Writers need to read other great writing. Public speakers need to listen to other speakers. In the same way, story sharers need to experience other stories firsthand. This means absorbing stories in a variety of mediums and industries.

- Read articles
- Watch movies
- Listen to podcasts
- Hear live speakers
- Enjoy novels

Immerse yourself in other great stories often. Notice what works for those storytellers and what doesn't. If your mind starts to drift, ask why. When did they lose your attention? What elements engrossed or distracted you? If you're enraptured by the story, take note of what the storyteller is doing to win you over.

As you encounter great stories, take notes. Collect these stories as an extension of your Story Library. This gives you an archive of stories and organizations to learn from. How do you think I came up with all of the story examples in this book? I spent years collecting them and documenting what made each one work.

Great athletes practice their sport over and over. But they

also spend time being inspired by legends of the sport and by watching their opponents get better. **Great storytellers experience the stories of others to refine their own craft.**

In Summary

- Sharing your story is meaningless unless it's experienced by your audience.

- The best stories transcend sharing information and transport the listener. A narrative connects with your audience and sparks an emotional response.

- Avoid distractions, doubt, or disconnection that could potentially spoil the experience.

- The best ways to entwine your storytelling with experience is to remember the story's context, aim for a specific emotion to trigger, and learn from your own experiences.

CHAPTER 8

CALL TO ACTION

Big Idea: Every story should point people toward a clear next step.

Follow the Frog

"*You are a good person.*"

That's how the video begins. The entire three-minute video is narrated in the second person, addressing you the viewer directly. However, this particular protagonist on the screen representing "you" is an unnamed 30-something, suburban white guy.

As the video explains, "you" are good because you do good things like conserve water, drive a Prius, give to charity, and recycle. You're someone who does their best to save the environment.

However, 20 seconds in, the video takes a turn. The main character wonders if he's not doing enough because the world is falling apart at the seams "and all you've been doing is yoga."

Then the main character learns that the rainforests are being destroyed at a rate of 32 million acres per year. This causes the character (and the viewers) to feel guilty, angry,

129

and like they've been apathetic for too long. He feels that he must do something about it.

The film takes another turn when the narrator explains "what you're NOT going to do."

- Quit your job
- Leave your family
- Fly to Nicaragua
- Find the heart of the rainforest
- Join a local tribe
- Earn their respect and trust . . . by getting branded by a fire-hot iron

The protagonist realizes that he's living out the "cliche gringo fantasy of becoming an honorary native." The screen shows examples of this movie trope as seen in *Laurence of Arabia*, *The Last of the Mohicans*, *Avatar*, *Dances with Wolves*, and *The Last Samurai*.

The video climaxes with the protagonist leading the natives in a revolutionary battle against the multi-national deforesters driving a bulldozer. Unlike those "gringo fantasy" movies, the revolution doesn't go well. It results in "you" waking up two days later in an El Salvadorian hospital missing two toes. And the story only gets darker from there.

Luckily, the narrator reminds you that these are things that you're not going to do. Because those things would be ridiculous. It's not how the world works. That still leaves the question: *can something be done to resolve the conflict of a dying rainforest?* According to the video, yes—something much smaller and more realistic.

Follow the frog.

The video shows a sequence of food products with the Rainforest Alliance frog sticker. These products are produced sustainably and "ensure the future of our rainforest." It's a much simpler solution than trying to go native and save the environment by yourself.

The humorous promotional video was created in 2012 for the Rainforest Alliance. It was written, edited, and directed by filmmaker Max Joseph, who has since gone on to create full-length movies. The video has been viewed on YouTube over 5.7 million times since it was uploaded.[30]

Beyond the funny concept and quality execution, the Rainforest Alliance video has one great strength that makes it stand out in storytelling—a strong call to action. Most of the video discusses what you shouldn't do, but it contrasts that with what you should do: Follow the frog.

The story gives viewers a clear action for what to do to make a difference in the environment—buy products that show the certified logo to ensure that the rainforest is being properly taken care of. Whether or not you buy these products, it shows the power of a meaningful call to action.

Your Objective is Action

When we read a powerful novel or watch a thrilling movie, we feel something. The realism of the narrative stirs our humanity and elicits emotion. As enjoyable as fiction is, it rarely holds a clear action for us to take as a next step. At best, we might

---

30   Follow the Frog, Rainforest Alliance (September 2012) [https://www.youtube.com/watch?v=3iIkOi3srLo]

recommend the book to a friend, or watch the sequel to the movie.

Organizational stories are different. **The most effective narratives have an end goal in mind and clearly call the audience to do something**. Fiction exists to entertain; nonfiction exists to educate or persuade. There are real-world connections to the messages contained within.

Simply put, **great stories inspire action**.

Lucky for you, these actions can be as varied as the stories we tell.

- It could be to start something like a diet or an exercise habit.

- It could be to stop something like smoking or bullying.

- It could be to buy something whether that's a product or a new idea.

- It could be to get involved by attending an event or volunteering.

In the words of author and storytelling expert, Bernadette Jiwa: "Marketing is the art of telling a story that moves people to act."

The action is up to you, but the story should be crafted to effectively convince your audience to follow through. Whether or not they act depends on who they are, but also how you connect them with your message.

One thing is clear: **your audience won't take action if you don't ask them to**. If you're not sure what you want them to do by the end of your email or blog post, they won't be either. Your success in convincing them is predicated first on your convincing yourself to include a singular and explicit call to action at the end of your story.

Figure out what action they should take and drive everything in your story toward that goal.

Cold Water Catches Fire

It's hard to trace the origins of a viral, grassroots effort. But if you dig deep enough, you'll find the challenge started with a golfer in Florida named Chris Kennedy. Chris took the challenge in July 2014 to raise funds for his relative, Anthony Senerchia, who suffered from amyotrophic lateral sclerosis.

Senerchia's wife took the challenge, too. She posted the video to Facebook where it was noticed by their friend Pat Quinn, who suffered from the same illness as Anthony. Quinn challenged another young man with amyotrophic lateral sclerosis. That young man's name was Pete Frates. And when Frates got involved, everything exploded.

Frates had been the starting center fielder for the Boston College baseball team and was pursuing a professional baseball career in Germany. But a routine baseball injury led to the discovery of his debilitating illness. On and off the field, Frates was an enthusiastic leader. So when he got word of the challenge that his friends were performing, he knew he had to tell the world.

Sitting in a wheelchair, surrounded by friends, Frates recorded the video of his challenge in the outfield of Fenway Park in Boston. He challenged the entire baseball community to support raising money to find a cure for his disease. After all, that disease famously bore the name of a professional baseball legend—Lou Gehrig.

With the gauntlet thrown, Frates' family raised a Gatorade

cooler full of ice-cold water and poured it over the young man's head. With that simple action, the ALS Ice Bucket Challenge went viral.

On social media, the video spread like wildfire. An endless list of celebrities pushed the challenge into the mainstream. In 2014, it was easier to create a list of people who *didn't* participate in the Ice Bucket Challenge than those who did. Because it was everyone—possibly including you.

Besides the celebrity endorsements and great cause, one reason why the Ice Bucket Challenge was a success was the clarity of its action. It was easy to understand how to participate:

- You recorded a video of yourself pouring cold water on your head.
- You posted the video to social media.
- You challenged three of your friends to do the same.

For the next several months, the Ice Bucket Challenge spread across our culture. Its story became an inescapable part of our zeitgeist. People invented creative ways to pour freezing water on themselves. The challenge spread to sports teams, big businesses, and late-night talk shows. There were even compilation videos of people who injured themselves while trying to complete the challenge. (Thus, bringing new meaning to the phrase: "Give until it hurts.")

All of that cold water added up.

An estimated more than 2.5 million Facebook videos were uploaded with the Challenge's hashtag. According to the ALS Foundation, it also sparked more than $220 million for disease research. That's a lot of cold showers.

The Ice Bucket Challenge's influence spawned an endless number of copycat charitable challenges: the Rice Bucket Challenge, Book Bucket Challenge, 22 Pushup Challenge, and Food Stamp Challenge, just to name a few. Every nonprofit saw ALS's success and sought to capture the same lightning in a bottle. But it's doubtful that any organization will ever replicate that first success. Being first made the Ice Bucket Challenge that much more impactful and unique.

In December 2019, Peter Frates lost his battle with ALS at the age of 34. His legacy lives on in the impact of the Ice Bucket Challenge. By leaning into the power of action, Frates and a community of others accomplished more than any of them could have individually.

Tracking Your Story's Success

One of the challenges with organizational storytelling is once you've shared your story with your audience the impact enters a metaphorical black box. After it's passed from your hands into the minds of the audience, the story is on the other side of the curtain. It's difficult to tell what your audience thinks of the story, if it sticks with them, and whether it had the desired effect.

That's why connecting every story to a tangible action is so critical. Establishing a clear next step provides you with tangible feedback on the relative success (or ineffectiveness) of your story. If enough of your audience takes that action, then your story can be considered effective. If not, then you know you have room for improvement.

Every story's action should be measurable. There should be a clear and reliable way for your organization to track the number of actions taken after each story. How many people registered for your event, signed your petition, or made a donation? This will never be an exact or perfect science, but it moves the act of storytelling from a vague concept to an impactful effort.

In case you're having trouble thinking of some trackable actions to attach to your story, here are just a few ideas:

- Buy a product
- Try a sample
- Visit our store
- Subscribe to our channel
- Donate
- Volunteer
- Attend the event
- Buy tickets
- Download now
- Refer a friend
- Make an appointment
- Schedule a demo

Know what action you want your audience to take. Understand how you can measure the number of people taking that action. When you combine those two things, you'll paint a more compelling picture of how effective your organization is at sharing meaningful stories.

Of Toothpaste and Persuasion

At the turn of the 20th century, Americans didn't brush their teeth. Only about 7% of the U.S. population cleaned their teeth regularly. Most of the dental products were powders hawked by door-to-door salesmen. Tooth health was largely ignored to the detriment of American smiles.

Then, everything changed.

At the time, Claude Hopkins was among the nation's most well-known businessmen and ad executives. He was approached by a friend with an innovative product—a toothpaste, rather than a tooth-cleaning powder. The product was called Pepsident.

Hopkins was skeptical at first. He didn't relish the idea of wading into the unpopular dental hygiene game and competing with countless sketchy salesmen. But his friend eventually wore Hopkins down and got him to invest. This would prove to be one of the best decisions of the ad man's illustrious career.

To make Pepsident profitable, Hopkins knew he'd need to convince most Americans to adopt a daily brushing habit. What Hopkins needed was a clear picture of what people would prevent by using toothpaste. He needed to put a bad taste in their mouth (pun intended) they couldn't ignore.

After some research, Hopkins found his negative motivation: plaque. He read that an unsightly film of plaque naturally builds up on teeth over time.

Pepsident's early ads encouraged people to feel their teeth for that film. Once people began to think about that, they couldn't stop. Then the advertisement gave a simple solution: brush every day with Pepsident. So people started doing exactly that.

Plaque hadn't bothered people before, but their awareness of it was bothersome. That simple cue made people feel self-conscious about the appearance of their teeth. That simple action created a problem best solved with Pepsident.

It wasn't the health benefits that sold Pepsident. It was how brushing made people feel about their teeth. Rather than a medical product, Hopkins positioned toothpaste as a "creator of beauty." And because this spoke to people's emotions (namely, vanity), it worked.

Adoption of daily tooth brushing skyrocketed from 7% to more than 65% of the population. Within five years of the product's existence, it became one of the most recognizable brands in the county—if not the world. Pepsident eventually became popular in Asia, Europe, and South America.

Toothbrushing went from an irritating anomaly to an assumed daily ritual—all because of one man's simple persuasion using an emotionally stirring narrative. Get rid of an unattractive smile by removing plaque by brushing your teeth daily; problem and solution.

The goal of your business' story isn't to inform or entertain—although those might be beneficial side effects. **Your goal is to persuade.** You can't persuade without a clear action. Figure out what you want people to do and why they should consider doing it. Then focus your story on that point.

An Unclear Story

We're not always accustomed to stories with a clear action step. Especially in comparison to fictional stories, ending your story with an ultimatum seems strange.

Without a follow-up, the Story Cycle stalls and the story dies. There are three common missteps: not including an action, including too many actions, or using an unrelated action.

No Action

Not including any action step in your story breaks the Story Cycle. **Without a next step, your audience will forget what they heard.** Giving them an action provides a path to internalizing the story. An action invites them to be a part of the story and to make it part of their own.

If you're persuasive enough to get your audience to the next step, they're invested. They'll remind themselves of the story because they need to justify to themselves why they took the action. If they've bought your product, attended your conference, or volunteered for your nonprofit, they'll use the story you told as a reminder of why they answered the call to action.

Including an action in each of the stories you tell makes it worth your time to share and worth your audience's attention to listen.

Too Many Actions

Sometimes we try to convince ourselves we need more options—the freedom to choose anything we want. But that's wrong. People want fewer options to pick from. Too many variables overwhelm us, freeze our minds, and stop us from choosing at all.

Don't make the mistake of cramming too many actions into the end of your story. Don't point your audience to a buffet line of products. Don't give them a vague notion of "getting involved" and hope they figure out what to do for themselves.

Be specific. Have a single action step in mind. Tell them to buy a specific product that connects to the story you just told. Recommend that they volunteer for a specific event by taking these explicit steps. Don't expect them to figure it out—not because they're not smart; their brains are just wired to conserve energy. **Don't exhaust your audience with too many options.**

Every call-to-action boils down to the choice between two options: taking your recommended action or not. If you've done your job, they'll understand why taking action is worth their time and what's at stake if they ignore your invitation.

Unrelated Action

The final mistake organizations make with their story action step is coming out of left field. An action invitation that has no relation to the story you just told tends to confuse people. And confused people don't make the best decisions or the best customers. Surprises are overrated; so, don't spring one on your audience when it comes to the call to action.

There should be a clear bridge between the story you've shared and what you're asking the audience to do. Typically, that's because you've told a pertinent example of someone like them who has used this very product or service.

Sometimes, that's a simple connection point for the organization to make. Sometimes, it's more difficult to find examples of those stories. But if you can't make a convincing relationship between your narrative and your next step, it's best to hold off on sharing the story.

How to Motivate an Audience

Make the Action Clear

There are a handful of famous novels with ambiguous endings—*The Life of Pi, The Handmaid's Tale, The Giver,* and

Great Expectations. An unresolved conclusion is acceptable in fiction because it's supposed to be art.

By contrast, organizational stories should be clear, not cryptic. Not every story will have a satisfying conclusion or be completely over—in fact, none should be since they are true stories that will continue to go on. But the actions you connect them to need to be unmissable.

If you don't know what action steps your audience should take, don't expect they will either. You're not trying to trick your audience into action or hope that they'll guess from a riddle. Your goal is to move them to action. The harder they have to think about what that step is, the less likely they'll take it. Eliminate any possibility of confusion.

Focus on One Action

In a famous scene in *The Matrix,* Morpheus gives Neo a choice between a red pill and a blue one. Choosing the blue pill will allow Neo to resume an oblivious and happy life as a pawn in a simulated reality. Taking the red pill will keep him aware of the truth.

You might think that Morpheus was providing two choices, but in reality, it was one choice—either action or inaction, knowledge or ignorance, remaining still or stepping forward. It was a binary of yes or no. You can confront your audience with a similar choice. (But maybe slightly less dystopian.)

People think they like unlimited choices. However, we're better off with fewer options. **The more options you give people, the less likely they'll decide at all.** Overwhelming people with too much variety paralyzes them. It's like ordering off of the Cheesecake Factory menu (which is longer than this book).

It's tempting to provide your audience with a litany of action steps. You think you're encouraging more participation if you give every available choice. But that requires more brainpower to sift through. And makes them less likely to take any action.

Do the work for them. Narrow down the choices. Make it a binary: either yes or no. Guess what? They might still say no, but at least it's clear what choice they're saying no to. By focusing each story on a specific action, you're helping people sort through the options you offer. Have different stories for each product you sell, service you offer, or way to get involved with your organization.

Connect the Action to the Message

Do you remember the end of *Monty Python and the Holy Grail*? The entire movie details King Arthur and his knights of the round table's search for the Holy Grail. They finally track down the chalice to a castle and summon an army to storm said castle.

Just as they're about to charge, a swarm of police drive in, arrest the knights, and unceremoniously end the film. If this wasn't a comedic movie created by a classically irreverent British comedy troupe, this would be considered a disappointing, and confusing ending.

Unless your business is a British comedy outfit, be sure to logically connect your story to the action you're offering. Make sure the two things fit together or risk leaving your audience more confused than motivated. **Your narrative should build toward the action you're going to offer.** Otherwise, you might end up with a flesh wound.

Call to Action

Make It Their Idea

Did you see Christopher Nolan's 2010 epic science fiction thriller *Inception*? No, it wasn't a dream. That movie was just confusing (but also entertaining).

In the movie, a group of corporate spies enters peoples' dreams using experimental military technology. At first, their goal is just to steal important information from their dreaming subconscious. But then they try to pull off something more dramatic—inception.

That's where they plant an idea into someone's dreams so that they adopt the idea as their own. It's a delicate process, like an organ transplant where the host might reject the idea if done improperly. And that's also the task you have when trying to get someone to accept your call to action.

There are two approaches to persuading them to take action: beat them over the head with your idea, or make them think it's their idea. You want to be clear and upfront with the action. But if they're going to follow through, then they have to adopt it as their own.

People don't buy stuff or donate to a cause because a company wants them to. People do those things because they want to. People need a justification for their actions, which an effective story provides. When done well, a narrative helps the audience own the action as their own.

Then again, maybe this is all just a dream.

Leave The Action Until the End

There's no way to quite be sure if anyone named Aesop actually lived. According to ancient Greek sources, he lived in the Greek city of Mesembria around 500 BC. From mentions in documents and histories, we can piece together a possible life of Aesop.

In this tradition, Aesop was an ugly slave who used his natural wits to free himself from a cruel master. From there, Aesop is supposed to have elevated himself to being an advisor and diplomat to a few royals. He used the power of stories to make his life better.

There are many legends of Aesop's eventual death. In one, the storyteller visits the Greek city of Delphi on a diplomatic mission. But he insults the townsfolk, who falsely accuse him of theft and toss him off a cliff. Despite his demise, Aesop still gets the last laugh because Delphi endures years of famine for their mistake.

Regardless of where, when, how, or even *if* Aesop lived, his stories and fables live with us today. An estimated 200+ fables and stories have endured over 2,500 years to the present— among them the tortoise and the hare, the ants and the grasshopper, the crow and the pitcher.

Perhaps the most notable feature of each fable is the moral shared at the end of each one.

- The tortoise and the hare taught us that slow and steady wins the race.
- The ants and the grasshopper taught us not to put off today's work for tomorrow.
- The crow and the pitcher teach us that Aesop liked using stories with animals in them.

What meta-lesson can we storytellers glean from Aesop's fables? The moral is to **leave the action until the end**. Aesop had a clear and relevant moral at the end of each of his tales.

The characters and events of the story led the audience persistently toward a direct conclusion.

That's why the missive of following the frog came towards the end of the National Rainforest Alliance's video. And why all Ice bucket Challenge videos saved issuing the challenge to friends and family for the end, too.

Inserting the action at the beginning threatens to disrupt the flow of the story and risks the audience forgetting what they were supposed to do by the end. So leave the action as a bridge that people can cross over into a transformative experience.

Speaking of which, that transformation is what we'll dive into in the final step of the Story Cycle.

In Summary

- Effective organizational stories have a specific action for the audience to take. Without a follow-up, the story is quickly forgotten.

- Your business should have a way to measure the outcome of these actions to judge the effectiveness of your storytelling.

- If there's no clear action, too many options, or an unrelated action step, you can bet on your audience not accepting the call to action.

- Clarity and focus on a single outcome is the best method for proper persuasion.

- Make the action relevant to the story you're telling and leave the action until the end.

CHAPTER 9

INSPIRE CHANGE

Big Idea: Effective organizational stories provide a blueprint for transformation in others.

The Merchant of Death and Peace

It's not clear what the newspaper headline said. But it came as a massive surprise.

The year was 1888 and a French newspaper ran an obituary for famed Swedish chemist Alfred Nobel. The article described Nobel as a "merchant of death." Among his 355 patents and inventions was dynamite, which was used in mining and engineering, but also warfare.

People around the world who read the newspaper were shocked. None more than Alfred Nobel himself, who was still alive. (It was actually his brother Ludvig who had died of a heart attack.)

Nonetheless, the 62-year-old Nobel was horrified at what he read—less angry at the newspaper's error, but its summary of his life. Was this his legacy—one of death and destruction? Something had to be done. So, this preeminent man of science set about rectifying his impact on the world. He was determined to change his story.

There is some debate as to whether this story is true or as fake as Nobel's first obituary. (The tale certainly bears a striking similarity to Mark Twain's "overly exaggerated" reports of death, reported to have occurred nearly a decade later.) But what happened after is undeniable.

Nobel's family built their fortune in industry. Alfred's father, Immanuel, was an engineer who ran munitions factories. Following in his father's footsteps, Nobel operated over 100 factories that produced explosives, earning him the nickname the "dynamite king."

This impressive network built Nobel a fortune worth approximately $280 million in today's figures. However, he was also an extremely well-educated man, spoke five languages, and read widely. Despite his line of work, Nobel even admitted to being a pacifist at heart. Alfred Nobel could not stand that his final legacy would be one of death and destruction.

It wasn't until his actual death in December 1896 that the world learned of his plans. Nobel's will outlined an awards program that would recognize contributions to physics, chemistry, medicine, literature, and peace. This decision wasn't without controversy. His relatives were upset about not getting more of his fortune for themselves. In his native Scandinavia, the citizens were upset that people from other countries would also be eligible for the awards.

But in 1901, the first of the Nobel Prizes was awarded. And Nobel's true legacy was cemented. More than a century later, over 600 awards have been given out to 900+ individuals and 25 organizations. These awards are given annually on December 10—the anniversary of Nobel's passing.

Most people now don't realize that Alfred Nobel invented dynamite or owned war munitions factories. That's more of a footnote in his story.[31] Nearly everyone around the world has heard of the Nobel prize. It's widely regarded as the most prestigious award in each respective field.

It's safe to say that Alfred Nobel inspired and empowered thousands of other stories because of his dedication to changing the ending to his own. In other words, he used his narrative to inspire transformational change—and you can seek to do the same.

Changing a Life

In his popular TED Talk and best-selling book, *Start With Why*, author Simon Sinek explains that people are motivated by the Why behind a cause more than the How or What.

- Our What is our product or service.
- Our How is the processes we use to provide these things.
- **Our Why explains our purpose or vision for a better world.**

Your business must make money to stay in business. You employ people because someone needs to do the work. You need an office building to facilitate the work and store all of your office chairs. These are the visible outputs of your business. But they're not the reason why you work. Your business needs something to offer people.

---

31   This is also a footnote. I hope you enjoyed it.

Your purpose is to serve your audience and hopefully improve their lives even marginally. You do this by offering a quality product or a service they can't find anywhere else.

This is where nonprofits and charitable organizations have an advantage—their mission of improving the world is front and center. Nonprofits 'sell' the value of their mission to donors who pay money to further the cause and get to be a part of the change.

Harvard Business professor Theodore Levitt is credited with saying, "People don't want to buy a quarter-inch drill bit. They want a quarter-inch hole."

Marketing guru Seth Godin takes this a step further by postulating that "no one wants a hole." Instead, they want the shelf that will go on the wall and the way the room looks when they put their books on the shelf. And the sense of satisfaction of knowing that they hung the shelf themselves. "People don't want to buy a quarter-inch drill bit," says Godin. "They want to feel safe and respected."

If all you sell is quarter-inch drills, then you'll go out of business as soon as people can find a better way to create quarter-inch holes or stop needing those holes in the first place. Your business is a means to an end. They'll do business with you as long as you provide value or earn their loyalty. But when you grow irrelevant or break their trust, then they'll find another source of value.

Home Depot sells plenty of quarter-inch drill bits and thousands of other home improvement tools. But people aren't shopping there so they can buy a tiny piece of shaped metal. People shop at Home Depot to make their homes look better and know that they did the work themselves.

Home Depot understands this. That's why they carry the products you'd need to do home improvement yourself.

They hire people who can answer questions about the tools you'll need. They host workshops explaining how to complete household tasks and share endless online content explaining those same lessons.

Home Depot knows that they're not in the "quarter-inch drill-bit" business; they're in the "more beautiful home" business.

In the same way:

- Nike doesn't just sell running shoes; they sell athletic gear that makes you feel capable of "just doing" the impossible.

- L'Oreal doesn't just sell shampoo; they sell beauty products that let you know that "you're worth it" to look good.

- Apple doesn't just sell devices; they sell the feeling of superiority that comes with owning the latest and sleekest technology.

- Walmart doesn't just sell, well, everything; they sell the peace of mind that comes from getting the lowest price.

- Coke doesn't just sell carbonated liquid; they sell the sense of community and fun that comes from drinking a cool beverage.

Don't just sell a product or offer a service—partner with potential customers to make their lives and the world around them better. Use your business model to continue to serve people. Many organizations are founded on that very principle—to help people change themselves and overcome a pressing issue in their life.

Storytellers Anonymous

Bill W. once had a promising future as a Wall Street stockbroker. He also had a major problem—he was a compulsive drinker. Bill nearly graduated from law school but was too drunk to pick up his diploma. He wrecked his marriage and his career with drinking. Alcohol landed him in a New York City hospital multiple times.

Despite his best efforts, Bill couldn't find the willpower to quit.

Bill was invited by one of his drinking buddies to join The Oxford Group, a religious organization that helped men find sobriety by teaching honesty, purity, unselfishness, and love.

Through The Oxford Group meetings and medical help, Bill eventually pulled his life together. It happened in fits and starts—a month or two of sobriety with the occasional relapse. Gradually, Bill found stability. He attempted to help other men in similar conditions, but none gave up alcohol.

Even with his newfound sobriety, Bill's alcoholism wasn't gone. The urge to drink was ever-present. But he discovered something that helped him to combat it.

During a business trip to Akron, Ohio in 1935, Bill faced a strong temptation to drink. The business trip wasn't going well. Five months sober, Bill was drawn to the bar of the hotel where he was staying. Suddenly, an idea hit him—he had to find another alcoholic to talk to. If he could only speak to another man who understood what he was going through, he could stay strong.

Bill contacted the local Oxford Group in Akron and asked if they knew any local alcoholics. Sure enough, they knew a guy.

That guy turned out to be Dr. Bob S. He began drinking

heavily while at Dartmouth medical school, barely managing to graduate. He married and opened his own medical practice, but nearly lost both to alcohol. His daily routine was to fight for sobriety until noon, after which he'd drink himself into oblivion, sleep until the next morning, and repeat the routine.

Dr. Bob S. reluctantly agreed to meet with Bill W. for 15 minutes to discuss their shared troubles. However, Bob was so impressed with Bill's experience that the conversation lasted over six hours. More importantly, Bob never drank again after that meeting. Bill ended up moving into the house with Bob and his wife to help coach Bob toward sobriety. And to keep himself in check, too.

The two men were so energized by the results that they wanted to help even more alcoholics. Bill realized that by helping others, he could keep his drinking in check. Through community and relationships, Bill and Bob believed they could make a difference.

The first two years saw Bill and Bob help about 40 other alcoholics. It took them four years to help their first hundred members. But those steady results propelled them forward.

In 1939, they wrote a book that outlined their twelve-step program. The book was called: *Alcoholics Anonymous: The Story of How More Than One Hundred Men Have Recovered from Alcoholism*. Years later, this book would become known as 'The Big Book' and their organization would adopt the name of the book: Alcoholics Anonymous.

Dr. Bob Smith died in 1950 of colon cancer. He was 71 years old and 15 years sober. At the time of his death, there were over 100,000 AA members across the country.

Bill Wilson passed away in 1971 at the age of 75. Although he had been sober for the last 36 years of his life, Wilson was a heavy smoker and died from complications of emphysema and pneumonia. Only two years later, sales of their Big Book surpassed one million copies. In 1999, Time Magazine listed Bill Wilson among their 100 most influential people of the 20th century.

Today, Alcoholics Anonymous has over two million members in over 100,000 active communities. The friendship between Bob and Bill has been detailed in books, movies, and a theatrical play. Their determination and reliance on one another have inspired millions to escape the crippling jaws of alcoholism.

Alcohol caused some serious conflict in the lives of Bill W. and Bob S. They fought tooth and nail to overcome their addiction, but it was only when they began giving back to others that they experienced transcendence for themselves.

Our businesses are the same—our ambitions and success will be short-lived if they're not aimed at some greater purpose or connected to helping those around us. **We have the power to help people become a better version of themselves**. Framing your business narrative in terms of what we do to help people is what makes the difference.

Stories Spark Transformation

Transformation provides a story with a resolution—a character that has finally overcome a troublesome conflict. Nowhere are these transformations on such obvious display as with reality television. Real or not, these shows understand the power of change.

For example, *Extreme Makeover: Home Edition* details a

family in need who gets a much-needed home renovation. The climax of the show nearly always features a bus or plywood sheets being moved out of the way to reveal the new home. It's a moment of pure emotion and joy—but it's also one of stark transformation.

As the family tours their new home (with tears in their eyes and speechless cliches on their lips), the show's editors deftly splice in shots of before and after the renovation. The finished home is always beautiful, but even more so in comparison to what came before. Because, shag carpet? Really?

Most home-building shows (and there are quite a few of them) end with the familiar before-and-after montage. The entire reason these shows are so popular, and why these families are so satisfyingly stunned, is because of the perception of change.

Homes aren't the only things that are transformed on reality television—plenty of shows also feature people undergoing change. Netflix's *Queer Eye* features a cast of gay men ready to makeover someone in a slump—with their expertise in food, grooming, home decor, and fashion. The show's five hosts help a deserving person with the means to improve their life for the better.

Even romantically-focused programs don't skimp on the transformation. Take *The Bachelor,* which is all about finding an eligible single guy and changing him into a newly-engaged man in only a few short weeks. Just add thirty insecure women into one location and stir.

Change is the central focus in each of these human dramas.

As we detailed at the beginning of this book, change is one of the four crucial ingredients to making a story. It holds if your organization wants to tell stories, you must offer things worth changing for. You must offer something of value to people that will affect a tangible alteration in their narrative.

- That could be the gym that helps people shed unwanted pounds and find inner strength.
- Or the hair salon that helps women rediscover their beauty and confidence.
- Or the grocery store that not only provides fresh food for your family but also recipes and tips for how to cook a nutritious meal.

Life change might sound daunting or unattainable. Keep in mind, that you don't need to drastically alter the course of your customer's identity to make their life better. Our lives are rarely transformed overnight by a single product or idea—not everyone is the author of *Eat. Pray. Love.*

More often, people's lives are made up of tiny, incremental changes that form a larger pattern. If your brand fits into that patchwork quilt, then you're a part of changing their life. For that, you'll have a loyal customer. **Any business that genuinely seeks to serve its community can tell stories of how they've inspired change.**

The Uninspiring Story

What's the quickest way to lose customers, lose trust, dry up inspiration, piss off employees, and cease the flow of decent stories into your business? Focus too much on money and yourself.

For every inspirational business that serves its community, there are a dozen examples of faceless corporations who got too big, too greedy, too selfish, too complacent and ended up going out of business for those very reasons.

People do business with companies they feel have their interests in mind. You've got to show people you care. This can be done through the stories you tell, but ultimately, this has to align with how you do business. Because **how you do business tells the loudest and longest-lasting story of all**.

- How you treat your customers tells a story.
- How you market your products tells a story.
- The price you charge tells a story.
- The salary you pay your staff tells a story.
- Your return policy tells a story.
- How long people wait on hold for customer service tells a story.

All of the interactions that people have with your business are pieces within a larger, unspoken narrative about your brand. These aren't explicit stories, but stories that customers create themselves. And unspoken stories aren't ones your business can control or contribute to.

What kind of stories are your business practices passively telling? Are you the guide in that story, or are you the villain? What stories do people tell themselves about your company? Is it one that will inspire them to change their life and continue doing more business with you? Or is it a story of how they're going to avoid you at all costs and tell their friends to do the same?

The stories we tell matter; the stories we inspire others to tell about us matter even more.

Stories That Inspire Change

It's great to talk about inspiring change, but what does this look like? What stories can your business tell to practically transform your community? There are endless narratives that might meet this goal, but here are eight examples for you to consider.

1. Testimonials

To testify to something means to bear witness. In the legal system, people are called to testify and provide evidence. Religious followers share their testimony of how they came to believe in their deity of choice. Writers use testimonials to interview subjects and compile biographies on historical figures.

In the business context, **testimonials are stories other people tell about us.** We can collect testimonials from customers and clients through conversations, surveys, or by encouraging them to leave us online reviews.

We hope these testimonials are positive but brace yourself for the negative feedback. If you get large enough, you'll eventually have some harsh criticism. You can't make everyone happy. Some people want to be angry and give you a one-star review online because they're bitter. Take solace that the rational among us can see through their poorly-written review and realize that the problem is with them.

Sharing these testimonial quotes—both written and in video format—are subtle ways to let your customers speak for you. You'll no doubt share the positive ones (we shouldn't give that crazy person any more attention), but people tend to trust a third-party perspective over what a business says about themselves.

2. Case Studies

If a testimonial is a bite-sized sample of a customer's opinion, then a case study is a full-on buffet. A case study is a more in-depth (it has the word study in there, after all) and focused story about a single customer and how you helped them with an issue.

This allows you to walk through the process from beginning to end and show how your business helped lead to a transformation.

- Start with an overview of their situation.

- Then focus on the problem they faced.

- Explain how they sought out your company and why they chose to do business with you.

- Tell them about the solution you provided for their specific problem.

- Then, detail the results and how your solution worked (hopefully it worked, why else would you be telling this story?).

Because they're longer and more detailed, save sharing case studies for people who have already shown an interest in your business. Share these on your website or other places people will spend more time reading—not on social media unless you're going to break it into smaller pieces.

Keep in mind, that not every business will benefit from the case study story format. These work better for service-based companies (think landscapers or home builders) and business-to-business providers (companies that sell to other companies, rather than individuals). But don't let that stop you from trying a case study to see if it works in your circumstance.

3. Before and After

The Partnership for a Drug-Free America once released a series of PSAs on the danger of illicit drugs. These ads featured, of all things, a man making scrambled eggs. It goes something like this:

> "This is your brain," says the generic-narrator man, holding up a single egg.
>
> "This is drugs," he says, indicating a frying pan on a stovetop.
>
> He cracks the egg into the hot pan where it begins to immediately sizzle.
>
> "This is your brain on drugs," he concludes. "Any questions?"

This campaign has been lauded for its effectiveness and cultural impact. It's been revived in different versions over the years. *TV Guide* named it one of the top 100 TV ads of all time. The PSA works because it's simple, clear, and shows a visual representation of what your brain is like before (whole) and after (scrambled) doing drugs.

We talked about why reality TV shows use the before and after images to quickly paint a picture of transformation. Even infomercials do the same thing—showing happy people with six-packs contrasted with a photo of their previously slubby and sad selves.

Before and After stories are ways to visually and viscerally demonstrate the transformation your business is capable of.

Paint a clear picture of what a customer's life is like without your brand. Contrast that directly with how this picture is changed when you enter the frame.

The Before scenario is when your customer's world is consumed by the problem. The After is when you've helped your customer achieve peace and happiness with a resolution. That dramatic transformation is where your story derives its power.

4. Community Impact

There are a lot of shoe companies out there. They vary in price point, durability, use, style, fit, and a dozen other different ways that aren't exciting to hear about in a story. Then there's Toms.

Regardless of whether you have a pair of Toms, you've likely heard of the brand. And I doubt it's because of how comfortable they are or because of they look. If anything, Toms shoes look ordinary. But the story behind each shoe is what sets Toms apart from a crowded footwear marketplace.

That's because Toms was founded on the "one-for-one" model (a term that they've actually trademarked)—for every pair of shoes the company sells, they donate a pair to someone in need. This might not seem significant for people who own dozens of pairs, but it has a profound impact on those in poverty who spend most of their lives barefoot.

The one-for-one model works—not just for creating a community impact, but also for growing a business. People like it when the companies they support are supporting others. It paints the narrative of a better world that they're a part of. It might cut into your profit margin, or cause you to charge more for your product, but it also helps you stand out from the competition.

That's also why this one-for-one model has been copied by several other companies, including Bombas with socks and Warby Parker with glasses. This directly connects the story of the business to the idea of a larger community impact.

Communicating community impact distinguishes your brand from others. Companies will have similar products or services but different track records with volunteering or donating to nonprofits. You don't even need community service built directly into your business model. Simply giving back to the world around you is enough to make a difference.

5. Founder Story

We've covered a few company origin stories in this book. These are effective ways of explaining your company's history and why it matters. An even better angle is putting a face on your company by telling the story of your company's founder (or founders).

Did you know that Proctor and Gamble—the titans behind the 200-billion-dollar consumer goods company—went into business together because they married sisters during the 1830s? It was originally their father-in-law's idea to start a company and merge their candle and soap-making skills. Hopefully, they gave him a slice of the company.

Bill Hewlett and Dave Packard founded a computer company in their garage well before Steve Jobs & Steve Wozniak—way back in 1934. And they decided on the order of their names in Hewlett-Packard with a coin flip.

Ben Cohen and Jerry Greenfield met while running (slowly) on the track in middle school gym class. They stayed friends through school until eventually decided to start a business together. They debated between a bagel restaurant or an ice cream business—and made their decision because start-up costs of ice cream were lower. You've probably already heard about P&G, HP, and Ben & Jerry's. But knowing what brought those two names together adds a personal element to each one. You can do the same with your business—even if it wasn't founded by two old guys with a silly backstory.

These stories are particularly effective for startups and entrepreneurs because those are sometimes the only stories they have. Just like with budgets and resources, new businesses have to operate lean and mean. The good news is that effective storytelling can help grow the companies beyond that point. As a research study on the subject of entrepreneurial storytelling points out:

> "Stories can be especially valuable for small ventures with limited financial resources, as the ability to tell stories and to have others retell your stories can become a means of creating resources."[32]

6. Team Stories

There's a company beloved by millions of Americans. However, it's a mid-sized regional company. It's in a dying industry (and a boring one at that). After closing branches and declaring bankruptcy, the company was bought by a conglomerate that sells cheap office printers. Even the

---

32   Lefsrud, Lianne and Jennings, Devereaux. *Being Entrepreneurial in Your Storytelling: An Institutional Tale.* (2013)

employees of this company don't even particularly like their employer.

On top of all that, the company doesn't even exist.

The company's name is Dunder Mifflin. And they sell paper.

In case you're not aware, Dunder Mifflin is the business featured in NBC's colossal comedy success, *The Office*. The show was successful because it showcased the lives and stories of the average American workspace, which just so happened to be a regional paper company in Scranton, PA.

Even after nine seasons, we still know so little about Dunder Mifflin as a company. It was just the setting, the backdrop—the context if you will. The real draw of *The Office* was the people who worked there—Michael, Dwight, Jim, Pam, Andy, Angela, Phylis, Creed, and the rest of the gang. They made Dunder Mifflin worth remembering.

This teaches us that often the people who work at your company can be more interesting than the company itself. Stories of transformation aren't just limited to the people outside of your organization. The people who work for your business are also a source of inspiration. Not because you need a reason to talk more about your company, but **because your colleagues also have stories worth telling**.

- Interview your coworkers or board members.
- Ask them about what makes their work meaningful.
- Learn how they came to get their current job.
- Find out what they like about the company and the culture.

You can also ask about their negative feedback, but perhaps more as a reference for how to improve, not as much for story fodder. Understanding ways to make your culture better generates even better internal stories.

These employee stories are especially good for recruiting, but they can resonate far beyond that. Hearing your team's narratives remind people your company is made up of people.

7. Customer Journeys

If you study marketing enough, you'll hear the term customer journey used an obnoxious amount. Marketers have made the brilliant realization that people don't immediately buy every product they see. Humans require a few interactions with a business before we trust them with our money. That process of deciding to buy something is called the customer's journey.

Some people research a company online first. Or if they're older, look them up in a phone book. We ask our friends about which plumber or florist they use. We visit a website and read online reviews—but mostly the one-star reviews. Only then do we make a decision.

Your company can smooth out this process by sharing examples of customer journeys. Find satisfied clients (possibly by searching through positive online reviews). Interview them and ask about how they came to do business with you.

- How did they hear about your company?
- Did they research any of your competitors?
- Were there hesitations to do business with you?
- What questions did they have about you?

Don't shy away from their hesitations. Addressing the barriers that might keep someone from working with you helps assuage their skepticism. People trust the opinions of their friends more than your business. **Telling customers' stories introduces them to another person they can trust on your behalf.**

8. Core Values

If your company values your customers and employees, you likely have a set of core values. Not every company can effectively value everything (as much as some of us might try). So which ones you prioritize describe who you are. **Behind each core value is an opportunity for a good story.**

Your values could include community service, diversity, transparency, the environment, inclusion, or something else on an infinitely long list. Find a story highlighting how you live out each one.

For example, among Whole Foods' core values is "Practicing Win-Win Partnerships With Our Suppliers." To support that, they've created a local producer loan program. This makes it possible for their food partners to remain in business and continue supplying their food. Their website lists partners who have taken advantage of the program.[33]

Talking about core values is a way to talk about your company and why you're big news, without coming across directly as overly self-interested. If you're not embodying these core values, telling stories about them might be a challenge.

---

33 Local Producer Loan Program, Whole Foods Market [https://www. wholefoodsmarket.com/mission-values/local-producer-loan-program]

The Cycle Starts Again

The beauty of the Story Cycle is that it's self-perpetuating. When your business uses great stories to change customers' lives to market your business, it inspires more people to do business with you, which in turn inspires new stories of life change.

When done properly, the Cycle keeps going around and around.

The thing about cycles is that they keep rotating—otherwise, riding a bike would be much harder. Except, the process isn't exactly a cycle, because it's not the same story spinning around. It's more like a spiral—it keeps expanding outward by inspiring new stories and life changes.

Once you've inspired life change in your customers, you'll naturally want to capture those stories. Then you'll again need to edit and share them. Those stories should be experienced by your audience and hopefully inspire them to act, leading to more life changes.

Rinse and repeat. Recycle and reuse.

This also means your work is never done. **There are always more stories to tell.** That's the blessing and the curse of your work. It's the privilege of your position—to help people and be entrusted with their stories to share with others.

In Summary

- Your ultimate goal in business is to improve people's lives in some small way. The stories you tell reflect that transformation.

- When done well, storytelling showcases the opportunity for life change. This inspires the right people to do business with you.

- The stories we tell matter, but the stories we inspire others to tell matter even more.

- Once you've changed someone's life for the better, they have a great story to tell. And it's time for you to capture that story—signaling that the Story Cycle has continued turning.

THE 3 STAGES OF THE STORY CYCLE

Not Throwing Away My Story

Ron Chernow had established himself as a rock-star biographer of some of the United State's most notable historical figures. He already published definitive works on American financiers J.P. Morgan and John D. Rockefeller. But Chernow was tired of writing about businessmen and wanted to broaden his scope into politics.

In 1998, he discovered the subject of his first foray into the government—a prolific and under-appreciated American legend. For more than six years, the biographer studied the prodigious writings left by this nearly-forgotten founding father. Chernow visited the island where his subject was born and held the gun that took his life.

Six years later, Chernow published the 800-plus page biography to much critical acclaim. His book won the National Book Critics Circle Award and the inaugural George Washington Book Prize for American history. It also caught the attention of a young playwright.

Lin-Manuel Miranda read Chernow's new book while on vacation with his family in Mexico. Miranda immediately saw that "hip-hop songs started rising off the page" and knew that he wanted to translate the story into the dramatic arts.

Miranda got his shot at this a few years later. Chernow attended a Broadway showing of Miranda's first play *In The Heights,* and the playwright invited the biographer backstage to chat. Chernow was initially skeptical about telling the story through the medium of hip hop. But Miranda's knowledge and passion for the subject eventually won him over.

Enough to the point that Chernow agreed to be a historical consultant as Miranda wrote the play. For another six years, the two collaborated on the structure of the story. Finally, in 2015, *Hamilton: An American Musical* debuted at New York's The Public Theater.

Hamilton's fame needs little introduction—16 Tony nominations and 11 wins, including Best Musical; a Grammy Award for Best Musical Theater Album; and the Pulitzer Prize for Drama. That does nothing to explain the pop-culture phenomenon *Hamilton* became, or how difficult it was to get a ticket to see the show.

It should be no surprise that *Hamilton's* content itself is rich with the idea of storytelling. The play's titular character is obsessed with cementing his legacy. He sings with his fellow revolutionaries about how people would eventually "sing the story of tonight." His beloved wife, Eliza, yearns to be "a part of the narrative," until she learns the secret of his affair and "erases herself from the narrative". The play's final number contemplates the questions of "who lives, who dies, who tells your story." The entire drama is dripping with storytelling tropes and tributes.

Alexander Hamilton lived quite a memorable story. Ron Chernow crafted this narrative into a lengthy biography. The book, in turn, inspired Lin-Manuel Miranda to write the most popular play of the 21st century. There's no telling how many subsequent stories *Hamilton* has inspired within the next generation. And it's worth asking ourselves what stories inspired the original Alexander Hamilton to live the way he did.

Stories are a self-perpetuating life force. The best stories are shared with others and inspire more stories in turn. The act of storytelling is the act of turning the wheel once more in an endless cycle.

The Snake That Eats Itself

The Ancient Greeks had a symbol that they called *ouroboros*, which means 'tail-devourer.' The symbol depicts a serpent eating its own tail, thus creating a circle—a self-cannibalistic loop that never begins or ends.

This famous icon isn't just well-known in Greece—it's made appearances across time and cultures. The ouroboros appears in ancient Egypt, Rome, India, Scandinavia, and beyond, all with different names and slightly new forms.

Regardless of when and where it shows up or what it's called, the symbol symbolizes roughly the same thing: the endless renewal and rebirth of eternity. The ouroboros is an infinite cycle of life, but also of death, fertility, and more. No wonder why the circle has become a stand-in for those same things—being represented with everything from wedding bands to *The Lion King's* The Circle of Life.

One of the few things older and shows up in more cultures than the "snake who eats his own tail" is storytelling. **The art**

of storytelling will never die; it's the enduring language of humanity. In the same way, the stories we tell have lives of their own. If we foster an environment for these stories to thrive, they'll not only last but give birth to new narratives.

Stories are an embodiment of the same things as the ouroboros: they're nearly infinite, they repeat themselves, and they often talk about life and death (and sometimes fertility, too). They're also all-encompassing and seem to show up everywhere. That's why it makes sense to think about storytelling as a cycle.

Even though the two halves of the Story Cycle are separated into the audience (the hero) and your organization (the guide), there are bridges that connect these two halves. Your organization and audience are intrinsically connected by the threads of the stories you tell. These bridges break the Story Cycle into three separate stages: Story Listening, Story Building, and Story Sharing.

The 3 Stages of the Story Cycle

Story Listening

To know what stories to tell, you've got to listen. But to have stories worth telling, your business should be improving people's lives. So, the Story Cycle ultimately begins at the intersection between Life Change and Capturing Stories.

If you're having trouble finding sources for good stories, look for where your business impacts people. Who are your loyal customers? What keeps them coming back to you? If your company has a customer service or client support team, they'll be the ones to ask.

Telling great stories begins with listening for great stories to tell. Our business becomes a part of people's stories when we help to change their lives. This is the phase when the audience hands off their torch to your organization. Try not to drop it.

Story Building

For stories to make an impact, they must be intentionally crafted and shaped. But what shape should these stories take? What is the point we're trying to land with each message? The answer to those questions lies in the action we want from our audience.

Effective stories have a point—they drive our audience to a clear outcome that can be tracked. Stories become effective through the practice of assembling and editing a narrative towards that call to action. We can't truly know how to build a story until we know what we want out of it.

These two pieces of the Story Cycle fit right in the middle—between listening and sharing. This middle is often overlooked and the more difficult piece to enact. Editing stories and tracking their effectiveness are no easy tasks. But they're crucial to keeping the Cycle going.

Story Sharing

Once you've collected and crafted a decent story, it's time to share. But you'll need to know who your audience is and how they'll be experiencing the story. This phase is where your organization hands the torch back to your audience.

This is the most visible touchpoint between the two Story Cycle halves. That's also why it's where most people focus their time and attention. Since you've gotten to this point of the book, you realize that it's only a piece of the puzzle. And it takes all of the pieces to form a complete picture.

All good stories must be experienced and that all depends on how they're shared. How you share the narrative impacts how it's received. Make sure it lands with a bang, not a whimper.

Maybe Everything is a Story

I'm going to end by directly contradicting myself. After all, change is an important part of the story process—so I'm allowed to change my mind while writing a book about storytelling.

Earlier, I unequivocally said that not everything is a story. Perhaps I wasn't completely right. Maybe everything really is a story. Maybe not every story gets full justice. Miss certain pieces from the Story Cycle and miss out on landing with the right audience. But that doesn't mean it doesn't have the potential to be a meaningful story.

What are businesses but stories? Without a unifying narrative, an organization is just a bunch of people who happen to sit in the same building or have the same logo on their business cards. Even that logo tells a small story by itself. **All companies have a story at their core**—some are just better at understanding and leveraging that narrative for employee productivity and marketing.

Most things in our society could be viewed as stories.

- Relationships are stories about what another person means to us.

- Families and friends are special to us because of their roles in our story.
- Countries and governments are man-made structures that exist in the minds of people. Their power comes from our willingness to believe in their story.
- Currency is just pieces of paper and round metal that only have value because we all buy into the story that they have value.

Human history is a collection of stories that are important to us as a society. There's no way to tell the entire story, but different pieces are louder than others because of what's important to us.

Each of these unconventional stories is full of characters, context, conflict, and change. Those elements of a story can be found when we look hard enough. Some are explicit and some are unspoken. **Perhaps everything is a story**.

If that's the case, not every story is heard, crafted, or told to its full potential. Not every story has an artist willing to dedicate their attention to elevating the narrative. Not every story is carried on by an individual or an organization. Not every story lives long enough to find an audience it loves and have little story babies.

If stories have living things, they need our care. Stories cannot survive without human attention. A forgotten story perishes. Not all stories deserve to be told or passed on. But there are enough worthy stories that aren't told. Plenty of stories to go around for those willing to put in the work to uncover them.

Never forget that humans benefit from the Story Cycle, too.

Stories depend on us for life, but we depend on them for meaning. Hearing the right story at the right time is enough to change a life. That's the power and responsibility you have. Use it wisely and enjoy the experience.

And they all lived happily ever after. Or something like that.

THE BIG IDEAS

1. Every true story has specific ingredients.

2. Stories have a natural lifespan that depends on their impact.

3. Your organization isn't the hero of the story—you get to be the guide for your audience.

4. Before you can tell great stories, you must listen for them.

5. You can't share a story in its raw form; you must polish it first.

6. After listening and crafting, a story is ready to be shared.

7. Your story must draw your audience into a memorable experience for it to make a lasting impact.

8. Every story should point people toward a clear next step.

9. Effective organizational stories provide a blueprint for transformation in others.

DISCUSSION QUESTIONS

Use these discussion questions to dive deeper into each chapter—either with your organization, a book club, a professional group, or on your own.

Chapter 1: Not Everything is a Story

- Do you agree with the premise that not everything is a story?
- Can you think of a story (either corporate or fictional) that highlights each of the four elements of storytelling?
  - Context
  - Character
  - Conflict
  - Change

Chapter 2: Stories Are Living Things

- Do you agree that stories are living things?
- What evidence do you have to support or refute this claim?
- What are other examples of stories that have endured in our culture?

- Which do you believe are more potent for changing lives—fictional or nonfiction stories? Why do you believe that?

Chapter 3: You're Not the Hero of the Story

- Who is the intended audience of your business' stories?
- How do you keep this audience in mind while telling your stories?
- What are some practical ways your organization can establish itself as the guide in your audience's existing narratives?
- What goals are you trying to achieve through storytelling?

Chapter 4: Capture the Story

- Have you ever tried listening for stories within your organization before?
- If so, how did this experience go for you?
- What's your preferred method for capturing stories?
- How can you intentionally learn to become better at this practice?
- Where do you currently collect the stories you hear?
- How do you think building a Story Library could help with your process?

Discussion Questions

Chapter 5: Craft the Story

- Do you normally think of drafting and editing as two different practices?
- How are they different from one another?
- What are your biggest challenges when it comes to editing a story?
- Why do you think it's important to edit a narrative before sharing it?
- Have you ever tried sharing an unedited story before?

Chapter 6: Share the Story

- What do you think of when you hear the term "storytelling?"
- What images, sensations, or emotions immediately come to mind?
- What are the most common challenges you've faced when sharing a story?
- Which are your preferred methods or platforms for storytelling?

Chapter 7: Create an Experience

- What are some examples of ways to invite an audience to experience a story?
- How does empathy play a role in sharing your brand's narrative?
- Which stories have felt most like an experience to you?

- What are ways you can intentionally experience more stories?

Chapter 8: Call to Action

- How do great stories inspire action?
- Can you think of a time that a story persuaded you to change your behavior?
- What are examples of actions your business could call an audience to?
- How can each action be tracked to gauge the story's success?

Chapter 9: Inspire Change

- How does your business potentially make someone's life better?
- Who are people that could give examples of these transformational stories?
- Which of the types of stories that inspire change could you try using first?

ACKNOWLEDGMENTS

I f you're like me, you skip the acknowledgments section of any book. (So I won't blame you if you do the same now.) Before writing a book of my own, I undervalued how important this section is. I never realized how many people besides the author contribute to making a book happen.

After publishing my first book, *The Original Storyteller*, I found a new appreciation for the acknowledgments. Because a lot of people helped make my dream of publishing a book into a reality. So when I started to write *The Story Cycle*, I intentionally set out to find people to include in the acknowledgments. I wanted to collect the insights and feedback of a variety of friends and colleagues. Because it's made this work better.

If your name is listed here, I truly appreciate all that you've done—directly or indirectly—to make this possible. Books don't come from individuals but from a community. My heartfelt gratitude goes out to everyone who includes me in their community or has agreed to be a part of mine.

Thanks to my writing group—John and Wesley Otwell, and Kevin Wong—who read pieces of this book and much more of my writing. You guys have been a constant source of improvement and fellowship. I appreciate you always being willing to read the rough drafts I share every month.

Thanks to the people who reviewed this book when it was in a much rougher form: Evan Chasteen, Brian Dodd, Mickey Mellen, Kevin Hendricks, Will Schmidt, Tim Walker, Jesse Wisnewski, Jenn Wilder, Tom Pounder, Jeanette Yates, Jerry Carnes, Ali Green and Brandon Carter. Your insights, suggestions, questions, and encouragement helped me to shape this book into something worth sharing.

Thanks to my friend Wes Gay for writing the foreword to this book. You're an exemplary example of a storyteller and someone I look up to in this profession. Thanks also to the brave folks who were willing to endorse this book: Brian Dodd, Hudson Phillips, Jamie Howard, Grant Glas, Ted Lowe, Kyler Nixon, Jono Smith, Vanessa Chase Lockshin, and Jesse Wisnewski. I appreciate the kind words and your willingness to lend me your support and credibility.

Thanks to my coworkers at GreenMellen for being a great organization that helps to tell stories for many other businesses. I couldn't have written this book without a team that supports and encourages creative work like this. It's a pleasure and privilege to work with you guys.

Thanks to the team at Lucid Publishing for making this book possible—Megan Poling, Casey Cease, John Cochran, and the rest of the team for lending your expertise to this book's success.

Thanks to my family for supporting me and encouraging me along the way. To my parents, Cady and Jerry, for teaching me about stories. To my sisters, Caroline and Rachel, for reading stories with me. To my in-laws, Bruce and Elaine, for helping make our family's story better. To my grandparents—Bob, Mady, Nannette, and Jimmy—for creating a legacy of stories that have inspired mine. To my daughter, Elise, for reminding me what's important in life and what it's like to have an imagination and dream big.

Most importantly, thanks to my wife, Victoria, for being a constant source of joy and love. You put up with countless hours of me tinkering with this book (and others). You withstood all of the random ideas and stories that I've shared with you. And you've done it with a smile and a helping hand. I'm unbelievably lucky to be married to you and still be friends.

Also by Robert Carnes:
The Original Storyteller

Stories are everywhere. They are the common theme shared by all people. They exist in every language, culture, time-period, and nation. Stories engage and entertain. They create emotion and empathy. Stories unite and connect.

But why? What makes stories so powerful? Why are they so universal? How is a good story able to penetrate the distractions of a busy world? What causes a story to activate the minds of people anywhere?

The Original Storyteller seeks to answer those questions through the lens of God's stories. He is the first and best storyteller. His stories reveal the essence of all great stories. Take the journey towards becoming a better storyteller.

ABOUT THE AUTHOR

Robert Carnes is a professional marketer, freelance copywriter, and the author of two previous books, including The Original Storyteller.

His career has included work in sports, nonprofits, churches, and a digital marketing agency, all focused on helping organizations tell better stories. He lives in Atlanta with his wife and daughter.